MW00578633

Fundamentals of Design

Understandig, Creating & Evaluating Forms and Objects

niggli

CONTENTS

CONTENTS

This book deals with formal research.

The aim of this book is to give designers
- an overview of the available forms
- to present a systematic structure of objects.

Because anyone who understands and can read the structure of existing objects can independently develop new objects methodically. This book is to be understood on the one hand as a collection and on the other hand as an inspiration for artists, architects and designers to arouse our curiosity and continue to amaze us.

In order to understand the book and to set the desired expectations, it is first necessary to distinguish between two terms. *Formal investigation* and *design* are not the same thing:
- formal investigation
  is the development of forms free from considerations of possible application.
- design
  is the development of forms taking into account external influences, e.g. a possible application or different manufacturing processes.

Four possibilities of form development are available to the creator.
- selecting objects
- modelling objects
- transforming objects
- combining objects

The processes of selecting, modelling, transforming and combining an object are equal processes in the design process and are not subject to a predefined order. Each of these processes is independent of the others and can be used on its own or in any combination.

The first two chapters, *Forms* and *Shaping Operations*,
summarise shapes and shape-giving operations into a collection
that has not been available before. Thereby
- shapes, objects in two- and three-dimensional spaces,
- operations, transformative and modelling
- terms from design

are presented and described.

The third chapter, *Evaluation Criteria*, deals with the influences to which
a shape is exposed and with which different evaluation criteria a shape
can be considered.

Consideration of objects
Up to now, formal-analytical investigations
- have been carried out from a functional point of view,
- connected with emotions that the forms evoke,
- and investigated according to their form-giving operations.

Functional and emotional criteria for describing shapes are evaluative or
comparative criteria that are essentially determined by the culture of the
observer. Unfortunately, this way of looking at things is not necessarily
comprehensible for people with different cultural backgrounds.

The previous approaches led to shapes and objects being charged with
meanings like: "Red is hot, stands for fire and passion".

Such statements are not formal descriptions; instead, emotional effects are
described. So in the example above, the effect of the colour red is described
in words, but the structure of the colour is not described.

INTRODUCTION

The knowledge of the culture-, situation- or context-dependent meanings of form and colour is an important topic in its own right in design and has already been dealt with intensively by several authors.

Describing complex forms in terms of their emotional expression or functionality is a legitimate way of "simply" "describing" them, but this attempt at describing form reaches its limits in cross-cultural works and quickly leads to confusion in terms of content.

An emotionally borne description of an object does not describe the object itself but the effect of the object on the observer. In order for objects to be described and explained in a universally valid manner it requires knowledge of a system within the world of objects.

In generative design, a distinction is already made between the intention of the designer, his technical description of the object or the form-giving operations and their design effect. For a computer can do less with "faster" as an object related attribute than it can with to increase the length of an object.

A general description and ordering of objects is needed to
  – understand the structure of surfaces
  – to name the most familiar shapes.

In order to understand a form, it is necessary to look at it analytically, to break it down into its constituent parts, with the aim of further optimising. It is noticeable that there are recurring forms, structures and patterns that can be named. Knowing these building blocks simplifies the work of every designer.

Shape-giving operations are not to be confused with the criteria with which forms are evaluated. Shape-giving operations are the tools of shaping.

An example should make the difference clear: compression and stretching are form-giving operations. For the subsequent evaluation of the operation, it is not the operation that is considered but the result. The proportions of the object are evaluated.

Further stretching or compressing create a better proportional relationship. Shaping operations can be divided into three groups
- Transform
- Modelling
- Combine

The difference between transformation and modelling lies in the way a form is constructed and processed:
- in the mechanical approach, objects are transformed
- in the mathematical approach, objects are modelled.

The point of view can be constantly changed in the design process. Both ways of looking at things are not mutually exclusive, but they can even complement each other.

The third point of the shaping operations, combining, works equally well for transformed and modelled objects. This means that several objects are intentionally and methodically put in relation to each other.

Relationships follow one or more rules, it is only the deliberate and application of relationships makes an object to a designed object. A trained designer is able to explain the relationships and their meanings. This is necessary so that a conscious and comprehensible further development is possible in the design process. This is especially true for large projects in which several designers and other team members from other disciplines can work together.

The relationships of individual bodies to each other are described by more detailed operations and can be very broadly diversified. The present collection focuses on a "technical" range of Gestalt-giving operations and offers a rough overview. A detailed collection of narrative relations is only touched upon here and will be considered separately.

"No admission without knowledge of geometry"
The alleged motto above the entrance to the Platonic Academy in Athens.

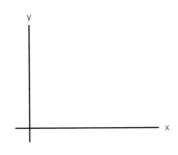

The development of objects. In order for an object to exist, it first needs a space. This applies to both 2-dimensional and 3-dimensional spaces.

In the world of design, a room has at least two dimensions. It has a height and a width. The concept of the coordinate system from mathematics makes this clear. The description of a two-dimensional space is represented with two axes, an X-axis (width) and a Y-axis (height).

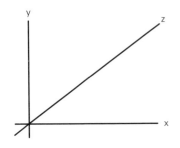

For 3-dimensional space, depth is added to width and height. The 3-axis coordinate system borrowed from mathematics, supplemented by the Z-axis (depth), visualises this understanding of space.

The coordinate systems are auxiliary constructions to better explain and understand object development and construction.

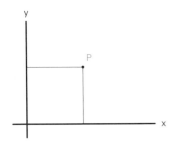

Point. A point is an auxiliary construction. A point is not a shape, it describes a property in a place. It can be, for example, the end of a line, the beginning of an edge or a turning point of a curve.

In practice, a point is made recognisable by a mark, in the example, an "•" marks the position and the name of the point should be "P". The dashed lines show the X and Y values on the respective axes.

Linie. A line is described by giving the line a beginning and an end point. In the example on the right, these points are each highlighted with an "•" and named P1 and P2.

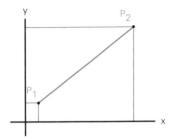

The analogy to mathematics is chosen for ease of understanding. However, this is not about mathematics but about understanding how universal objects are developed.

Area. If another point P3 is added to the line and the points P1 and P2, P2 and P3 and P3 and P1 are connected, a closed surface is created. In this example a 3-corner.

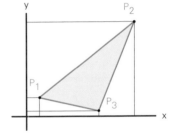

4-corner. Any number of points can be added and thus any number of corners can be developed.

For the sake of simplicity a regular surface is represented, so the 4-corner shown is a regular 4-corner or square, or also a square.

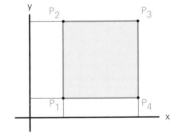

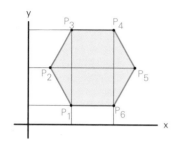

6-corner. Two further points in the arrangement shown here to form a regular hexagon.

This principle can be continued at will. Irregular combinations are listed in the detailed consideration of individual n-corners.

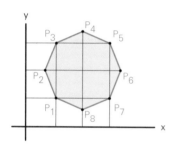

8-corner. The higher the number of corners, the more the representation of a regular n-corner resembles the representation of a regular circle. For this reason, no further enumeration of regular n-corners will be given.

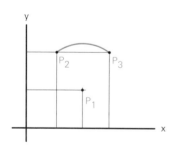

Circle segment. For a curve, no matter what kind, at least three points are needed to be able to describe it unambiguously.

In this example it is a segment of a circle. Here a centre point (P1), a beginning (P2) and an end (P3) of the curve are needed.

Circle. Three pieces of information are necessary to describe a circle. In the example on the left there are

- the centre (P1)
- the radius (distance from P1– P2)
- the information that each further point to be set should have the same distance to P1.

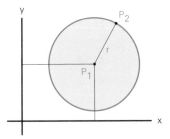

Spline in the plane. A curve with two points is shown on the right. Both points have one vector each, vectors V1.1 and V2.1, which are parallel to each other and of equal length here. In the next illustration, each point has two further vectors V1.2 and V2.2, each pointing in the opposite directions of the first vector in each case.

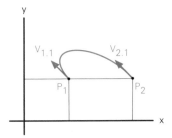

Vectors. Can be thought of as a force pulling on a line in one direction. If the anchor is at the end of a line, then there can only be one direction for the pulling force. If the anchor of a vector is on a line, two vectors can point in different directions in the anchor.

Vectors

- describe with their own direction the direction of the shaping of the line
- describe with their length the degree of deformation of the line
- are always tangential or colineal to the line
- are always tangential to the line.

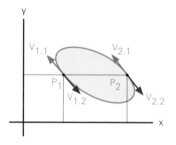

Closed splines. The vectors of each point can extend in any direction within the plane of representation, to give the line any length and shape. Splines can create open and closed lines. If 2 meeting vectors are not tangential to each other, corners, peaks and edges will apear. This is a way to decribe complex lines very simple and clear. Seemingly "free" lines become readable, explainable and reproducible as splines.

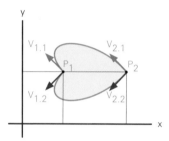

From the flat plane into three dimensions. With the Z-axis a flat space becomes 3-dimensional. For the unambiguous definition of a point, the third coordinate, the Z-value, is added.

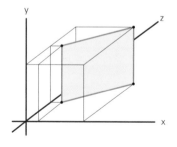

2-dimensional plane in space. A 2-dimensional plane in space is a plane that does not have to be congruent with one of the three planes. The plane penetrates at least one of the planes of the coordinate system.

Planes can exist in a 2-dimensional space just as in a 3-dimensional space. The difference lies in the environment (the coordinate systems) in which it is located.

3-dimensional plane in space, simply curved.
A 3-dimensional plane is not flat, it has at least
one curvature. The position of a simply curved
plane can be determined by the contour. The
plane has no thickness and therefore no volume.
However, the plane needs a space that has a depth
in order to exist.

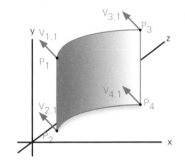

3-dimensional plane in space, 2-fold curvature.
A plane in space can also have several curvatures
in different directions.

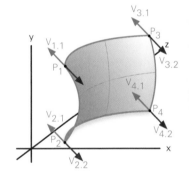

Detailing of a plane. For complex surfaces with
different curvatures, a plane can be represented
and controlled using several splines. The spline
can be understood as a "cut" through the plane.
The aim is to represent a shape with as few splines
as possible. This facilitates the later modelling of
the surface

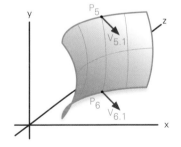

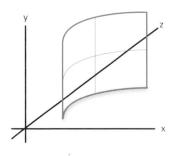

Representation as a net. A surface created using splines can also be represented as a "wireframe model". The surfaces that are stretched between the splines follow the vector specifications in the anchor points of the individual splines.

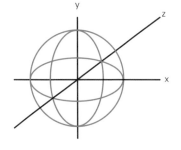

Representation as a grid. In this way closed surfaces that form a volume can be represented.

In the example, three round closed splines can describe a network that represents a sphere in the eye of the beholder. On each of the three planes, which are perpendicular to each other and thus describe the space, there is a circle with its centre at the origin of the coordinate system. This is the simplest wireframe model of a sphere. Meshes and grids can be used as simplifying representations for complex surfaces and volumes.

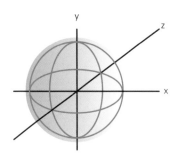

It can be summarised: Lines that cross each other develop nets, which in turn can represent surfaces. If a surface is curved and closed, the surface becomes a grid. The shape is controlled with vectors that are fixed in an anchor, which in turn controls a spline.

This kind of form understanding allows forms to be developed and analysed quickly. For the designer, this kind of form understanding offers advantages for his analysis and further development of complex forms.

Another advantage is the daily use of the computer: The designer now has a mould construction model with which he has quick and intuitive access to common CAD software without limiting his shaping skills.

Within the framework of the formal investigations in this book, only the
- 2-dimensional space
- 3-dimensional space

will be considered.

In mathematics, other multi-dimensional spaces are described. It is certain that in the future multi-dimensional spaces and their objects will play a role in design. Additive manufacturing processes already allow this today. Today, they still play a subordinate role in everyday design. They are only touched upon in the current collection.

Nothing

In design, "nothingness" is an important design element.

A comparison with a theatre stage quickly shows why this is so. When there are two actors on a stage and no one else in between and no props are placed, the colloquial expression is "there is nothing".

Of course it is not like that. There is no "nothing" in the world that surrounds us. Something is always there, but no senses are stimulated. "Nothing" in design means that there is no additional stimulation that generates attention.

Details of a design are comparable to theatre actors on a stage, there are the main actor(s) and some supporting actors. They are all surrounded by the stage on which they act. The stage (not only) forms the spatial framework of the action, it is also the platform that sensitises the observer to a certain mood and attunes him to the actors. This is done with stylistic devices that support the actors in their performance.

The comparison should make clear that the interplay between details and a less sensory-stimulating environment are equal parts of a composition. The designer thus directs the attention of the observer and supports the recognition and experience of the design intention.

Plane and surface

Both are abstract objects. A plane is a special form of the surface. The plane points in all directions and has no end. It is flat and nowhere touches itself. It will only serve as a support in further considerations in order to be able to better grasp and describe other objects. A relative of the plane is the surface. A surface is finite, has at least one edge and can be curved.

Point

"A point is what has no parts", said Euclid. Thus the point in the world of objects is very comparable to zero in the world of numbers.

A point is an object
- without area
- without volume.

For the designer, a point is an abstract object. This means that in the place of the point there is no surface or volume but special properties, usually construction aids:
- a selected location,
- the starting or end point of a line,
- a corner or a point of intersection,
- the centre of a circle,
- the slope of a function,
- the centre of gravity of an object.

Although the point has no area or volume, it can be recognised and determined. Observers "construct" a point via relationships that are recognised in the shape. A natural object, an "X" or a small circle, is used to mark a point.

Line
"The line is a length without width"
Strictly speaking, the line is also an abstract object, since the line, like the point, has no surface or volume. The line describes a connection between two points in a surface.

A straight line is the shortest connection between two points. Unlike in mathematics, where straight lines can also be infinitely long, the designer knows straight lines with a beginning and an end.

A curve is a curved or bent line. It has a high point that is not on the straight line.

One wave has at least one high, one low point and a turning point.

For designers there are planar curves and planar waves, i.e. lines that are located in 2-dimensional space. Curves and waves can also be curved in the third dimension.

In order for the viewer to see a line, it is given a thickness for display purposes and thus, strictly speaking, becomes a surface.

Curves

Designers rarely define their shapes using mathematical functions. There are four terms from the curve discussion in mathematics that a designer should add to his or her language use, as they greatly simplify the discussion and development of splines. Especially when one thinks that many CAD and drawing programmes are easier to use with this understanding.

1.

2.

The following components of a curve are necessary to describe a curve:

1. high point:
   rising tangent becomes the
   decreasing tangent
2. low point:
   decreasing tangent becomes the
   rising tangent

3.

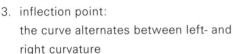

4.

3. inflection point:
   the curve alternates between left- and
   right curvature
4. saddle point:
   is a turning point with horizontal
   tangents

A selection of curve examples:

5. parabola
6. tangent curve
7. sine curve
8. curve with undercuts

5.

6.

7.

8.

1.

2.

3.

4.

5.

Spiral (curve)

In the following, spirals are considered in the plane their shape can be transferred into 3-dimensional space at any time.

The first group of spirals consists of a curve that moves circularly around a centre, changing its distance from the centre.

1. Archimedean spiral:
   uniform rotation with a linear movement
2. logarithmic spiral:
   uniform rotation with an exponentially growing linear motion
3. Fermat spiral/parabolic spiral:
   the distance between the windings reduces constantly, but never touches
4. Galilean spiral:
   Compared to the Archimedean spiral the distance per turn increases
5. hyperbolic spiral:
   in mathematics it is considered an inversion of the Archimedean spiral
6. Fibonacci spiral:
   quarter circles are drawn into the respective squares and tangentially connected

6.

Spiral (straight)

This spiral is a sum of distances that moves in a circle around a centre and changes its distance from the centre in the process.

1. Archimedean spiral of distances: this schematic representation of lines can be created at any angle

2. Fibunachi spiral: two representations with different distance distributions of a Fibunachi spiral

This form of representation can be implemented with any spiral (curve).

1.

2.

2.

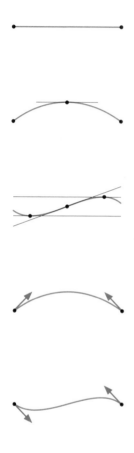

Spline

Is a special way of constructing a line or a curve. Splines are curves that are developed or described via knots and vectors. The word "spline" comes from the English language and means "slat". Ship-builders fixed the spline at any number of prede-termined points (knots) and then bent the spline in such a way that controlled curvatures were created with a minimum of bending energy. This is how ship hulls were made from individual boards (straw battens).

The nodes of a spline can be
- – end points
- – saddle points
- – turning points

of the curve, and the vectors are aligned accor-dingly to create the desired curve. Vectors are the force needed to transform a straight line into a curve. The anchors (red dots) make modulating the spline particularly intuitive.

Nodes can be at
- – arbitrarily defined points,

because, for example, another component already has a certain position and shape and is related to the planned spline.

This understanding of splines makes working with complex curves simple and intuitive.

Bèzier-Curve/Spline

The Bèzier Curve takes its name from Pierre Bèzier, who worked in computer-aided design at Renault. However, it was developed by Paul de Casteljau, who in turn earned his living at Citroen. Bèzier and de Casteljau developed their models independently of each other.

1.

For a better distinction in their construction you can see on the left the illustrations of a curve with vectors and in comparison the same curve in two different Bèzier curve models.

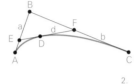

2.

You can choose between
1. basic spline
2. quadratic and
3. cubic Bèzier curves.

3.

to 2.   Put simply, the point "D" draws the curve in which the point "D" on the line d moves from left to right, while the point "E" on the line a (from "A" to "B") and the point "F" (from "B" to "C") on the line b.

to 3.   For more complex curves, points "B" and "I" slide on their respective line.

Today, this form of curve description is carried out by computers in the background.The boundary of an area means that the area ends here.

1.

1.

1.

Different types of boundaries are possible. The simplest is the edge, which can be straight or curved. Corner and point are special cases.

1. corner:
   A corner is formed from two non-tangentially lines.

2. edge:
   An edge is
   - the end of a surface,
   - created from two non-tangential surfaces.

3. vertex:
   A point arises
   - from a non-tangential winding of a surface around a point
   - in the non-tangential meeting of 2 or more surfaces at one point.

2.

2.

3.

Corner, edge and vertex are not limited to either
2 or 3-dimensional spaces. They can occur in both spaces,
e.g. an edge can be a curve lying in space.Corner, edge
and tip are among the important features of design, as
the consideration of a surface is often carried out over its
boundaries.

It can even go so far that the surface becomes a supporting
actor and the edge the main actor, as is often the case in
cars with the gaps between two sheet metal parts.

Whoever designs a surface should always mention
the edge of the surface in his design activity.

Boundaries of a surface are characterised by the fact that
there is an abrupt change of direction in the edge or in the
surface. This change of direction can take place in a point,
in a line as well as in 2-dimensional and 3-dimensional
space.

The abrupt change of direction causes at least two surfaces
to collide. In special cases, the edge does not go through a
surface, but only over a part of the surface. In this case, the
edge ends in a flowing transition or a point.

BOUNDARIES OF A SURFACE

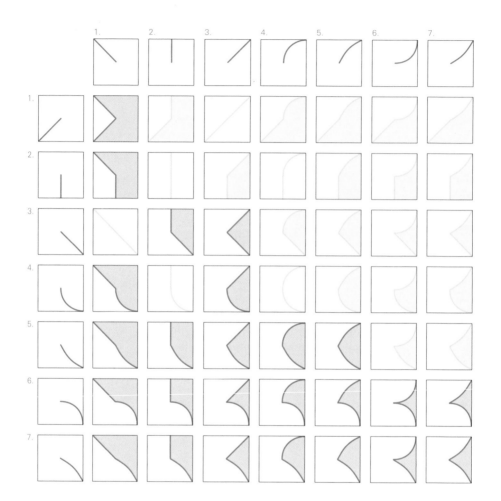

One corner, one edge (shown in cross-section)

A corner is not a closed object. A corner is created by
the non-tangential meeting of two lines. These lines
can be straight lines or curves. If two surfaces meet
non-tangentially, they form an edge. The surfaces can
also be curved.

The matrix to the left represents the principle combination
possibilities of two lines or surfaces (viewed in cross-section) that abut each other. The numbered lines are the basic
elements that are combined. The dark coloured areas are
the different combinations and the light coloured areas are
the double combinations.

The coloured areas can be read as both positive and
negative objects. The gaps show which combinations
do not result in a corner because the basic elements
meet tangentially. Crossing lines do not result in any
further variants and are therefore not pursued further
here.

The property of two lines or surfaces that meet and form a
corner or edge is described below and represents the basic
connections:
1. obtuse angle
   (angle greater than 90° but less than 180°)
2. right angle
   (angle 90°)
3. acute angle
   (angle less than 90° but greater than 0°)
4. curve tangentially obtuse
5. curve tapered
6. curve tangentially tapered
7. curve tapered

BOUNDARIES OF A SURFACE

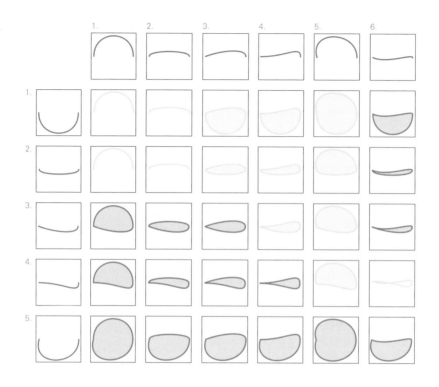

Objects with one corner

Objects with a corner are created from two
curves, where one end of each curve either
- meet at an acute point
- butt against each other
- run together once tangentially.

The end of a line can be tapered in different ways:
- tangential
- curve blunt
- pointed curve
- curve very acute.

Thanks to this overview, it becomes clear how
limited the possible combinations are in principle.
Only in the detailed elaboration will the different
appearances become clear.

BOUNDARIES OF A SURFACE

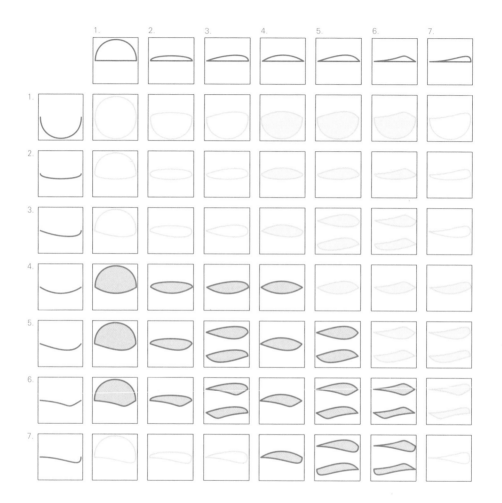

2-corner convex

The basic shape of the 2-corner consists of a curved and a straight line. As shown in the top horizontal panels. Furthermore, a 2-corner can be developed from two curved lines that do not converge tangentially at their respective ends.

There are the following possibilities how a curved line develops a corner with another line:
1. at right angles
2. a curve with a blunt taper
3. curve tapering to a point

Since a 2-corner has two corners, each consisting of two lines that meet, which in turn have three possibilities of meeting and these variants can be combined, the matrix on the left could be derived from this.

2-corner objects can be combined due to the combination possibilities
- symmetrical
- asymmetrical.

When two asymmetrical lines are combined, two different possibilities arise.

BOUNDARIES OF A SURFACE

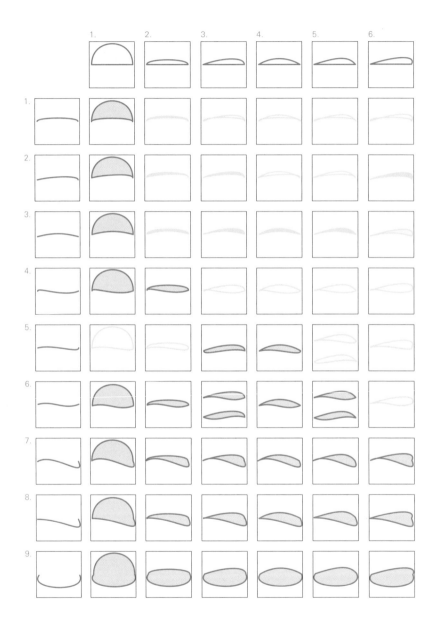

36

2-corner concave

In 2-corner convex the respective edge
guides are added to a growing object.
This is in contrast to the matrix 2-corner
concave in which reduced objects are created.

There are the following possibilities
how a curve can meet a corner:
1. tangentially obtuse
2. tapered
3. very acute
4. bluntly tapering

For concave 2-corner objects
- symmetrical and
- asymmetrical objects can be created

In order to create an object with two corners,
the two lines must not intersect. If two lines
intersect, the object is considered to be two
touching objects, each of which is already a
variant within the matrix.

Of course, convex and concave corners can
be combined, as exemplified in rows 7. to 9.

The two main groups of surfaces
- Polygons
- Polynomials

A polygon is characterised by the fact that it has corners. A corner consists of two lines that are not tangent to each other.

The polygon can also be called a n-corner, where "n" stands for any integer number. The best known simple n-corner is the 3-corner. In this collection, only n-corners up to 8 corners are treated in more detail. Shapers can increase the number of corners as they wish.

The polynomial is not to be considered here in its mathematical definition. For the designer, a polynomial is a surface without corners. Objects that will immediately come to mind are the circle, the oval or the ellipse.

Closed spline objects can be either polygons or polynomials and are colloquially referred to as "freeform". They are provided in all common CAD software with different creation methods. The "freedom" of "freeforms" exists in the design and consideration phase because the contour of the surface can be determined almost arbitrarily by splines. These surfaces are calculated and described as mathematical equations within the software. Designers, outside of generative design, very rarely bother to work with these equations. They regard these shapes as "free forms". Here they are defined as spline objects.

"Basic form" surface 3-corner

When examining shapes and bodies, one inevitably asks oneself the question of basic bodies. If you like, a 3-corner can be called such a basic body. Because no matter which polygons are considered, one will find that every polygon can be subdivided into 3-corners.

If a 3-corner is subdivided with an arbitrary straight cut, 3-corners are always created directly or indirectly. If a 4-corner is created by an arbitrary cut, a certain cut (a cut that forms a straight line between two corners not lying on an edge) will divide the 4-corner into two 3-corners.

"Basic form" circle segment

Polynomials have a curve. Ideally, it is a segment of a circle. This segment can be divided into two pieces of cake, each of which consists of a segment of a circle (half a lens) and a 3-corner. It is possible to subdivide this lens further. This creates cake pieces that can be subdivided again, and a lens and a 3-corner are created again. Thus, the circle segment with two corners (half a lens) and the circle segment with three corners are to be considered equally as basic bodies.

If the curve consists of a spline, this spline can be described via functions. The individual segments between the high, low, saddle and inflection points can be considered separately and form basic elements with their own properties depending on the function. The vectors in the nodes then determine the curve shape.

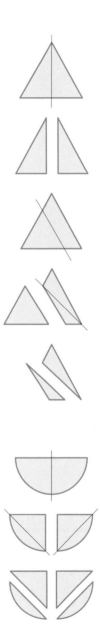

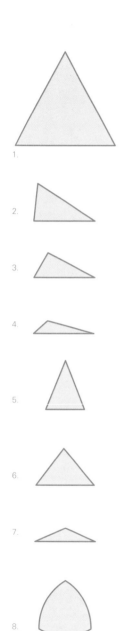

1.

2.

3.

4.

5.

6.

7.

8.

3-corner

A 3-corner is a simple polygon. A polygon is a closed line in a plane. Polygons can be divided into planar (lying in a plane) and non-planar (lying in space). We do not consider intersecting polygons (polygons in which the line intersects). For a designer, these are two separate simple polygons.

A polygon can be equilateral or equiangular. If there are two sides and also equal interior angles, one speaks of regular or iregular polygons. In the following, polygons are named after the number of their corners.

The 3-corner is the simplest figure in the plane, bounded by straight lines.

There is the

    1. equilateral 3-sided corner
    2. irregular acute-angled 3-corner
    3. irregular right-angled 3-corner
    4. irregular obtuse-angled 3-corner
    5. isosceles acute-angled 3-corner
    6. isosceles right-angled 3-corner
    7. isosceles obtuse-angled 3-corner
    8. Reuleaux`s 3-corner

4-corner

A 4-acorner has two diagonals, if both are inside the 4-corner it is convex. If one diagonal is outside, the 4-corner has a concave corner.

A 4-corner can be divided into two 3-corners, since the sum of the corner angles in the 3-corner is always 180°, a 4-corner has a sum of the corner angles of 360°.

The different possibilities of a 4-corner are:

1. square
2. rectangle
3. kite 4-corner
4. rhombus
5. convex 4-corner
6. tangent 4-corner
7. trapezoid
8. isosceles trapezoid
9. parallelogram
10. chordal 4-corner
11. concave 4-corner
12. concave kite 4-corner

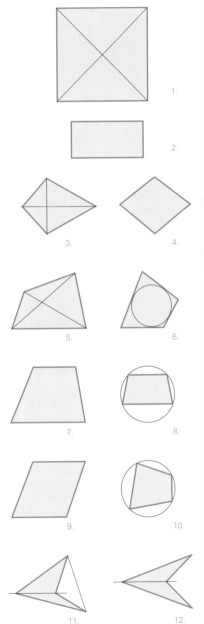

1.

1.

2.

3.

3.

4.

5-angular

A 5-angular is also called a pentagon (old Greek for 5-angular).

All sides of a 5-sided corner can be the same length, in which case it is easy to see that a 5-sided corner is only a variant of an isosceles 3-sided corner. An isosceles 3-corner is rotated at its tip in five equal steps so that its legs are congruent.

Variations of the 5-corner:

1. regular 5-corner,
   with a circle circumscribed
2. irregular 5-corner,
   circumscribed with an ellipse around it
3. irregular 5-sided corner,
   several sides are different in length and angle to each other
4. concave 5-corner,
   at least one corner points inwards

5-angular parquet

Particular attention should be paid to parcours with
- congruent
- convex

5-angular in a plane.

In 1918 Karl Reinhardt described the first 5 types of parquetry. In 1968, the mathematician Richard B. Kershner found three more. These 8 were supplemented by another one by Richard E. James III in 1975.

By 1977, Marjorie Rice discovered 5 more types. In 1985, Rolf Stein discovered type 14 and in 2015, thanks to special software, Casey Mann and Jennifer McLoud discovered the most recent parquetisation to date.

Tiling is grouped into types,
- if the same tiles can be parquet can be parquetised
- if tiles contain formal variants, the parquetry has the same structure.

Dark clarifies a tile,
Medium outlines the tiling pattern,
Light represents the parquetry.

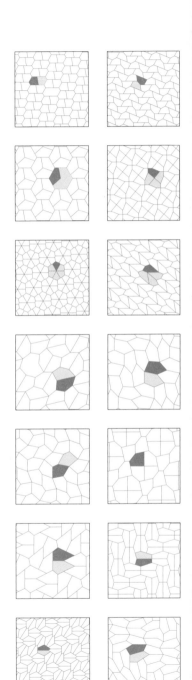

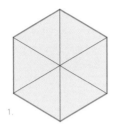

1.

2.

3.

4.

5.

6-corner

The 6-corner is also called hexagon (Greek for six and corner). Its best-known form is the equilateral regular hexagon, in which all sides are the same length and the angles of the sides to each other are the same.

Other forms of the hexagon are also possible
1. regular hexagon
2. kite-shaped hexagon
3. irregular hexagon
4. concave 6-corner
5. concave equilateral 6-corner

6-corner parquet

Further parquetisations are possible
and have not yet been investigated.

N-corner (7-corner/8-corner ...)

The more corners you give to an equilateral regular n-corner, the more the object approaches a circle.

If the shape has arbitrary edge lengths, it is often useful to reduce the complex shape into simpler shapes and to understand it as an addidition or subtraction of different simpler n-corners. Often, 4-corners and 3-corners offer themselves as building blocks.

Circle

A circle is a regular polynomial, its area is closed with a line, whose points are all at the same distance from a common (mean) point. All points lie in a plane. The distance of the points to the centre is described as the radius.

In everyday life, the point is represented as a circle, but this has purely practical reasons, because a point without surface cannot be seen, so in most cases the point is marked with an "X" or a circle, but this does not mean that the circle is a point.

Ellipse

The ellipse is one of the conic sections, just like parabolas and hyperbolas.

An ellipse can be constructed quickly and neatly by fixing two rice sticks on a piece of paper, knotting a string into a loop and placing it around the two rice sticks, the string should have a larger circumference than the two rice sticks stand apart. Tighten the string with a pencil and guide the pencil around the two rice sticks to create an ellipse. The average distance between the points on the ellipse remains at a constant distance from the two rice sticks.

Fortunately, in practice the designer has access to appropriate drawing software. If he works with hand and pencil, it is best to draw a "compressed" circle. This is done by creating a horizontal x-axis and a vertical y-axis that cross in the middle of their respective lengths. Mark an intersection point on the x-axis to the left and right of the origin at the same distance, and do the same on the y-axis, whereby the distance to the origin is smaller or larger than that on the x-axis. Connect these four marked points with an even curved line.

Any oblique cut through a cone with a circular base will produce an ellipse as the cut surface.

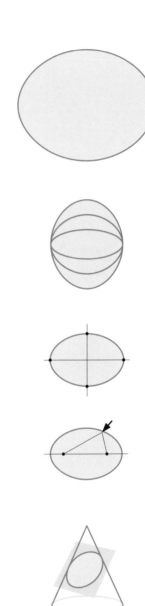

47

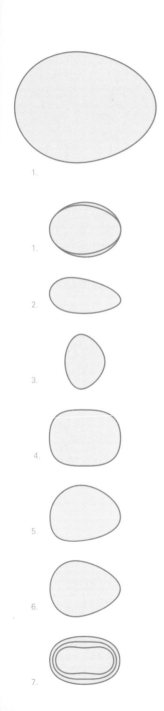

1.

1.

2.

3.

4.

5.

6.

7.

Oval

Oval is the Latin word for egg and describes a flat round convex figure.

There are symmetrical and asymmetrical ovals. It applies that a closed convex curve that can be continuously differentiated and lies in the plane is called an oval. However, this description does not cover objects that are called ovals and consist of segments of a circle, because their curve is continuously the same in places.

Ovals can be composed of circular arcs and straight lines, but these ovals are very inhomogeneous in their lines, which is why they are not considered here.

1. ellipsis and oval in comparison
2. irregular oval
3. elliptic curve
4. lamellar oval
5. unsymmetrical oval
6. Cassini curve
7. different Cassini oval

There are like the Cassini curve/oval still Lemmiskates, the Szegö curve, but today designers only use mathematical functions.

48

Closed spline objects

Closed spline objects can have a wide variety of shapes

1./2. be axially symmetrical about one or more axes

3. have one or more corners

4. be organically shaped

4. have n-corners with curves

5. be a combination of convex and concave lines

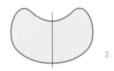

All these bodies have in common that they have at least two nodes from which a maximum of two vectors can span the line in each direction. Convex-concave interactions can occur.

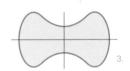

In the future, closed splines will certainly be the subject of the development of most new grades and determinations.

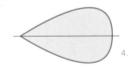

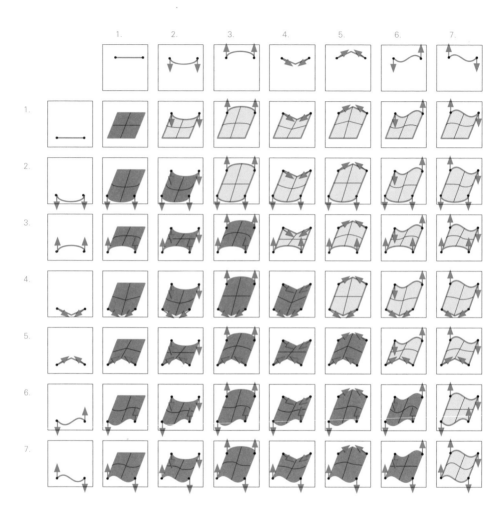

Areas in space (point with a vector)

Surfaces in space have no thickness and therefore no volume but they circumscribe a volume. If the surfaces are open, this means that every place in the room is accessible from every other place and is not made inaccessible by the surface.

Theoretically, all the solids listed in the chapter solids can be converted into a surface object in space by opening the closed volume to a surface object in space. This type of enumeration creates a confusing number of variants and distorts the overview so much that it is not shown.

A surface is determined by the direction of its vectors. The direction of the vectors determine the degree and type of deformation.

If the surface course is determined over two edges the following courses are possible
1. plane - plane
2. plane - curved
3. plane - angular
4. plane - wavy
5. curved - curved
6. arched - angular
7. arched - wavy
8. angular - angular
9. angular - wavy
10. wavy - wavy

The red arrows control the horizontal edges.

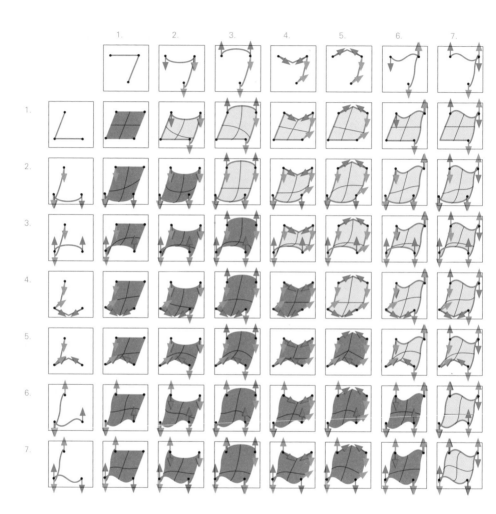

Areas in space (point with 2 vectors)

In this matrix, one width and one depth are combined. There are considerably more combinations possible at this point than shown, you can easily develop them yourself in the same scheme.

Each edge is assigned its own vector and has been assigned its own colour. Blue vectors for the width and purple vectors for the depth should clarify the corresponding assignments when reading.

It can be clearly seen how the surfaces not only curve or deform in one direction but how the surfaces are deformed in both directions of their original plane.

It becomes clear how the surfaces develop a complexity that is at the limit of clarity. A further increase in complexity is no longer achieved.

The red arrows control the horizontal edges.
The blue arrows control the vertical edges.

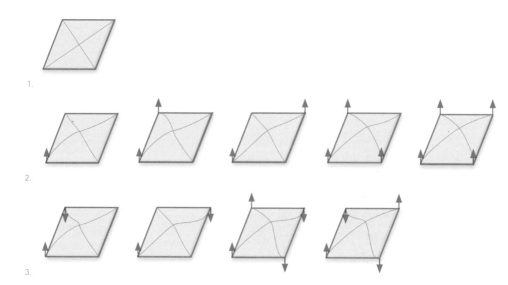

1.

2.

3.

Areas in space (the third vector)

A vector does not necessarily have to determine the edge at a contour, a vector can also have a direct influence on the area between the contour.

In the matrix only variations of this vector are considered, but of course the procedures of the two previous investigations can be combined with this one.

However, this does not necessarily result in new constellations, as partial areas of these combinations can be derived from those already depicted.

As is easily recognisable, all vectors can also be individually aligned in detail. As a result, high points, turning points, low points or edges and peaks are more or less distinct, but this is not new for the investigations into the basic structure of the respective surface courses.

A further increase in the number of vectors per point makes no sense, since all 3 vectors cover the 2-dimensional and 3-dimensional space.

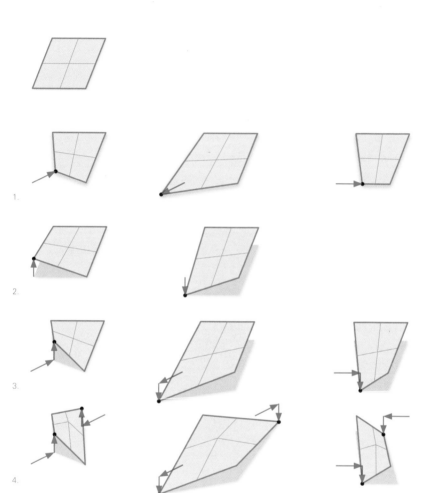

1.

2.

3.

4.

Move a point

The position of a point determines the contour of a surface just as much as the associated vector does.

The position of a point can be placed anywhere in space and thus influence the surface with manageable steps.

1. within the surface
2. perpendicular to the surface
3. combined displacement inwards
4. combined displacement outwards

The displacement of the point can be calculated with all vector investigations presented so far.

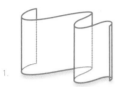

1.

Control surface, unwindable (simply curved) surface

A ruled surface is an unwindable, simply curved surface. This means that at every point of the surface it is possible to lay a straight line that is completely contained in the surface. The word rule is derived from the Latin term regula and means rod or ruler.

2.

Using a sheet of paper, simple unwindable surfaces can be created and controlled. Without bending, compressing or stretching the paper, the enveloping surfaces shown on the left can be created.

2.

Unwindable surfaces always have a rectilinear part, the generatrix. The generatrices can be parallel or meet at least at one point:
    1. cylindrical surfaces
    2. conical surfaces

Unwindable surfaces can be
    – closed
    – open

2.

Conoid

A conoid consists of ruled surfaces. A straight line can always be laid out flat in the ruled surfaces.

1. straight circle conoid
2. straight circle conoid
3. hyperbolic paraboloid
4. Plücker conoid
5. Whitney umbrella
6. parabolic conoid

The enumeration of two- and multi-shelled hyperboloids has been omitted, they are considered as two separate bodies in the design.

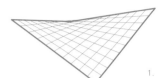

1.

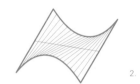

2.

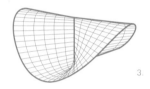

3.

4.

5.

6.

Screw surfaces

Screwing surfaces can be divided into
- standard screw surfaces and
- circular screw surfaces.

Both have the basic structure in common. They have an axis around which a meridian is screwed. The axis and the meridian can each be a straight line or a curve.

1. meridian-circle screwing surface
2. circle-screw surface
3. helical surface closed
4. helical surface open
5. meridian-parabola screw surface

Ray surface

Object 3. and 4. also belong to the group of ray surfaces. This means that a straight line (ray) of a curve is displaced along
- shifted
- rotated
- screwed

along a curve. The surfaces described are determined by the designer, unlike in mathematics, the line (ray) is not endless.

Single-flat

Are objects with one face and one edge.

Simple development of a one-surface ribbon.
1. tape
2. turn one side of the ribbon 180°.
3. connect both ends

1.

Further variations of one-surfaces are created by
- the number of rotations (180° + n x 360°)
- the contour of the pattern
- the variation of the width of the tape.

2.

3.

4.

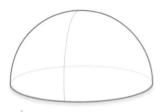

1.

Spherical segment

A spherical segment is a section of a sphere. When cut in a plane, the section forms a circular disc.

The section can be done

1. in diameter
2. above the diameter
3. below the diameter
4. as a curve
5. several times as a ring
6. several times as a segment

A spherical segment consists of a double curved surface. The same curvature exists at every point of the surface.

2.

3.

4.

5.

6.

Unwindable (double curved) surfaces

Double curved surfaces have two different
curvatures at one point. These surfaces are
divided into

1. saddle surface, concave surfaces
2. dome surface, convex surfaces.

1.

More complex double curved surfaces can
again be divided into individual saddle and
dome surfaces.

The versions shown can also be read as path
objects. A curve forms the cross-section and
is guided along a second path

2.

Minimal surfaces

Minimal surfaces have a three-dimensional contour. The smallest area that can be stretched between these contours is called the minimum area.

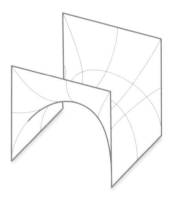

It can be observed in stretched materials or in
soap bubble experiments. Minimum surfaces are
the result of a previously determined contour. The
surface curve is the result of the requirement to
create the smallest possible area between the
contour.

The resulting surfaces are special
versions of double curved surfaces.

KNOWN SURFACES IN SPACE

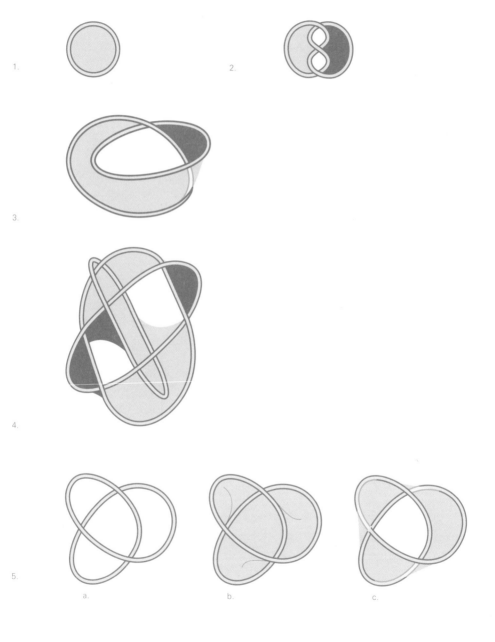

1.

2.

3.

4.

5.

a.

b.

c.

Seifert surfaces

Seifert surfaces are named after the mathematician Herbert Seifert. They describe a bounded surface that can be orentised by a node or an entanglement.

The edge of the surface can be described as a ring. The surface spanned in between can be compared with minimal surfaces, but it is developed in several stages with a complex algorithm.

The richness of variants of the Seifert surfaces is only limited by the possible variants of the nodes.

1. ring that spans a surface
2. Hopf link, a ring with an area comparable to an area comparable to a double helix between which a Seifert surface is stretched
3. two rings between which the Seifert surface is stretched
4. Borrmaic ring, which spans two surfaces between three rings
5. cloverleaf loop
   a. without Seifert surface
   b. with Seifert surface
   c. with Moebius strip

Volumes enclose a closed space, they separate an interior from an exterior volume. In contrast to this the known surfaces in space do not separate one volume from another. These areas are surrounded by one single room. The surrounding volume that these surfaces require has no formal influence on the surfaces or the object.

As in 2-dimensional space, there are also bodies with different complexities in 3-dimensional space. Thanks to the third dimension, more combinations are possible for the development of different objects.

These groupings represent the most common combinations. Due to the different properties of the individual bodies, they can also be assigned to different groups. The groups of bodies have logical connections to each other, which become clear through their common transformational operations.

Unfortunately, the group of polygons occupies a disproportionately large volume in this collection. This is because polynomials today show a manageable variance and are still an extremely young group.

"Freeforms", as they are also called, will continue to evolve and become easier to study thanks to CAD programmes that quickly display complex formal relationships. In this field, practicable groupings are still being developed.

Sphere

The spherical surface is a doubly curved surface where every point on the surface has the same distance from the centre of the object. This distance is described as the radius.

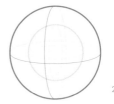
1.

1. the spherical surface can be seen from the inside as well as from the outside.
2. if the surface has a thickness, it is called a spherical shell.

The spherical shell can be understood as the product of a subtraction of a small sphere from a large sphere. This assumes that the objects each have a mass and do not just consist of a surface with a thickness of zero.

2.

The consideration of whether a sphere is solid or should be a spherical shell only plays a role in form-giving operations that show the interior of a sphere.

For the formal consideration and determination of a surface, the mass of an object plays no role.

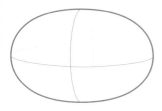

Ellipsoid

An ellipsoid is a body of revolution resulting from the rotation of an ellipse about its

1. vertical or
2. horizontal central axis.

This produces in each case a

1. rotational ellipsoid
2. triaxial ellipsoid.

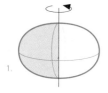

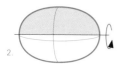

Ovoid

The ovoid is formed by the rotation of an oval around its longitudinal axis. The translation of the word "ovo" from Latin becomes the word "egg" in German.

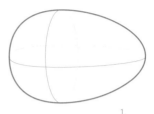
1.

Ovoids come in different versions
1. elliptical curve
2. Laméian oval
3. lamellar oval
4. Cassini oval

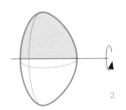
2.

Rotating a non-symmetrical oval results in a rotatinssysmetric shape, thus this type of shape development is excluded for an unsymmetrical oloid.
5. an unsymetric oloid
    is created by modelling.

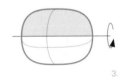
3.

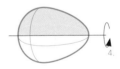
4.

5.

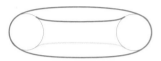

Ring

A ring is formed by the rotation of any cross-section around a centre point. The position of the centre of rotation can be positioned as desired.

The cross-section of a ring can vary in:
- size
- shape

Possible characteristics of a ring.

1. scaling ring,
   the ring consists of a smooth transition between at least two cross-sections of different sizes

2. morphological ring,
   the ring consists of a smooth transition between at least two different cross-sections

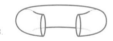

3. ring segment,
   the rotation of the cross-section is less than 360

4. body of rotation,
   the axis of rotation of the cross-section intersects the cross section

5. rotating cross section,
   parallel to the rotation of the cross section, the cross section is rotated around its own pivot point.

Possible cross-sections can be regular, convex, concave or even irregular.

1.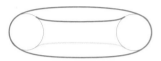

2.

3.

4.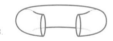

5.

Moebius strip

Compared to a single-flap tape, the single-flap volume has a cross-section with one face and at least one edge.

Suitable cross-sections have
- at least two edges
- edges that behave identically to each other

Examples of suitable cross sections are

1. symmetrical lens
2. equilateral 3-corner
3. square
4. n-corner
5. Reuleaux's equilateral 3-corner
6. Reuleaux's inspired equilateral 4-corner
7. Reuleaux's inspired equilateral n-corner

It should be noted that the rotation within the band is chosen in such a way that the surface is rotated further by the angle α with each revolution.

Further variables
- the bending radius of the band can be regular or irregular
- several belts can be combined
- the cross-section can be transformed.

1.　　2.　　3.　　4.　　5.　　6.　　7.

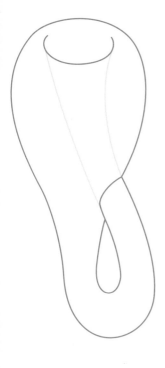

Klein`s bottle

In 1882, the mathematician Felix Klein discovered a non-orientable surface. The outer surface is indistinguishable from the inner surface, comparable to the Möbius strip, but without an edge and without penetration.

The tube penetrates its own wall and is turned inside out so that the surface merges without forming edges.

The illustration to the left presents only one possible variation, since the cross-section of the tube can be deformed at will.

Strictly speaking, Klein`s bottle does not belong to the closed volume bodies, because the volume inside the bottle is easily accessible from the outside.

The labyrinthine character of the volume development offers a lot of scope for future formal investigations, since its production has only become manageable with today's manufacturing methods.

Cylinder

A cylinder can be developed in two ways.

- shifting:
  The base surface is shifted in its vertical,
  both surfaces are combined with surfaces
  with another surface to form a closed
  volume.
- rotation:
  A profile is rotated around a standing axis.

1.

A cylinder consists of a bottom and top surface
and a jacket.

1. straight circular cylinder
2. cylinder section
3. oblique circular cylinder
4. tube
5. cylinder with rotating section

2.

2.

The possible base surfaces for a cylinder can
be divided into the 2-dimensional objects as
already described.

3.

4.

5.

Cone

A cone consists of a base surface and a tapering lateral surface. If the cone has a circular base and its apex is in the perpendicular of the centre of the base, it is called a straight circular cone.

1. truncated cone
2. oblique circular cone
3. cone with any base
4. pointed circular cone
5. blunt circular cone

1.

2.

3.

4.

5.

Sphericon

A sphericon can be developed from any regular n-corner. The n-corner is rotated 360 around its central axis so that a regular body of revolution is created. All sphericons have in common that their lateral surface is completely unrollable and that the sphericon has at least one edge and no corners.

4.

1. cone is developed from a regular 3-corner by a rotation
2. the volume is halved perpendicular to the floor and through the tip,
3. one half is turned until both cut surfaces are congruent again,
4. the two halves are congruently joined.

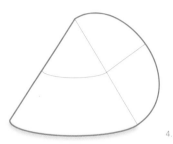
1.

The edges of the rotating cross-section can also be regularly convex or concave.

2.

5. - 11. a selection of different regular cross-sections

3.

5.

6.

7.

8.

9.

10.

11.

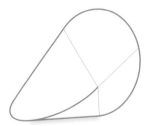

Oloid

The oloid is a special form of the sphericons.

The oloid was discovered by Paul Schatz in 1929. The oloid is the envelope of two perpendicularly intersecting circles whose centres are penetrated by the other circle. The oloid has two edges but no corners.

1.

The surface of the oloid consists of straight lines running from one arc segment to the other. If you place it on an inclined plane, the result is an unrolling image as can be seen at the left, this is also the complete lateral surface.

Paul Schatz wanted the oloid to be understood as a plausibility reference for the inversion kinematics he founded, which he developed from the discovery of the convertible cube.

The oloid can be varied in length and diameter by spacing the arc segments.

When unrolling an oloid, one obtains its complete mantle surface (1.).

Steinmetz body

The Steinmetz body is a sectional body consisting of at least two perpendicularly intersecting cylinders. They are named after the American electrical engineer Charles Proteus Steinmetz.

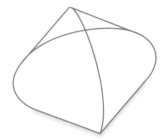

The Steinmetz bodies are also called bicylinders (two interpenetrating cylinders) and tricylinders (three cylinders interpenetrating each other at right angles).

The concept for shape development allows for further variants, conceivable are
- different (in size and shape) cross-sections for the cylinders
- more than three cylinders interpenetrating each other
- Cylinders that intersect at irregular intersect at irregular angles

These other variants are based on Steinmetz bodies.

Gömböc

The name Gömböc is derived from the Hungarian word gömb (ball, dumpling, fatty). This body was discovered by the two Hungarian mathematicians Gabor Domokos and Peter Varkonyi in 2007.

A three-dimensional body that has only one stable (mono-static) and only one unstable equilibrium position is called a gömböc. This refers to a specific shape,

Variations are not yet known.

Compared with a standing man from the nursery days, the Gömböc has no additional higher mass inside, the Gömböc consists of a constant, equal density. Due to its shape, the Gömböc always finds its only stable equilibrium position. In nature, a very similar shape is found in the Indian Star Tortoise. Its shell is an approximately monostatic body.

Polyhedron

Polyhedron means many-sided and comes from
ancient Greek. A polyhedron consists exclusively
of straight planes (faces), e.g. a cube. Bodies with
curved surfaces are not polyhedra, e.g. a cone.

Polyhedra can be divided into groups, which are
often named after a person.
- Platonic solids
- Archimedean solids
- Catalan solids
- Johnson solids

Some polyhedra are represented several times.
Thanks to their properties, they can be assigned to
several groups.

Some polyhedra are shown with one of their
folding templates. The folding template is used
for a better understanding of the structure of the
body. The folding templates always represent only
one of the possible folding templates.

Tetrahedron

A tetrahedron is the spatial closed arrangement of four equal 3-corners. The reflection of three 3-cornered faces on the fourth 3-corner creates a deltahedron.

1. regular tetrahedron
2. truncated tetrahedron
3. blunt tetrahedron
4. pointed tetrahedron
5. irregular tetrahedron
6. deltahedron
7. Reuleaux tetrahedron

1.

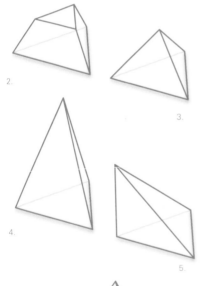

2.

3.

4.

5.

6.

7. front view

7. side view

Pyramid

A pyramid consists of an n-corner as the base and a number of 3-corners corresponding to the number of edges as the lateral surfaces. These lie against each edge of the n-corner and form a common tip, the pyramid tip.

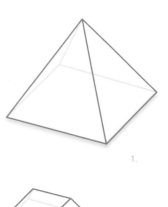

1.

A pyramid with a square as the base was depicted. The base is the part of the pyramid that gives it its name: a square pyramid. The previously presented tetrahedron is a pyramid based on the base of a 3-corner.

2.

Pyramids are divided into the following principal variants.

1. regular pyramid
2. truncated pyramid
3. blunt pyramid
4. pointed pyramid
5. irregular pyramid
6. octahedron, bi-pyramid

3.

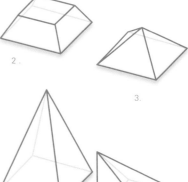

4.

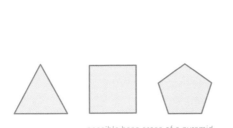

possible base areas of a pyramid

5.

6.

81

Cuboid

A cuboid consists of six faces, where the opposite faces are equal and parallel to each other. All faces of an edge are perpendicular to each other.

There are cuboids where
1. all edges are the same length
   the base and side faces are squares,
2. have two different edge lengths
   but a square base area,
3. have two different edge lengths
   and two square side faces,
4. have three different edge lengths
   so they have no square faces.

1.

2.

3.

4.

Prism

The structure of a prism consists of a base
surface and a top surface; all other surfaces
are referred to as the lateral surface.

The respective base surface consists of a
regular polygon. The number of corners is
freely selectable.

Regular prism:
Here all corners are touched by a circumscribing
sphere. In the case of a cuboid, the sphere is on
the inside and touches every face.

Tilted prism:
The cover surface is displaced in its plane,
thereby the surfaces of the mantle become
rhombus-shaped.

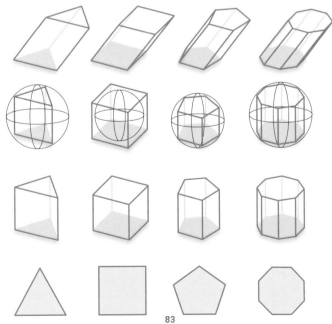

KNOWN VOLUMES

development of an anti-prism

anti-prism

diagonal
(2-cornered)

trigonal
(3-cornered)

tetragonal
(square)

octahedron
(square)

uniform antiprism

8-cornered

straight antiprisms

8-cornered anti-prism

Anti-Prism

In the case of the anti-prism, the cover surface is rotated around its centre by the value n. Then the corner points of the respective base and top surfaces are connected in such a way that equal 3-corners are created on the entire surface. Two variants can be created:

- – straight antiprisms, the lateral surface of which consists of equal 3-corners.
- – uniform antiprisms, the lateral surface consists of equilateral 3-corners.

Tetrahedron and octahedron can be assigned to the group of antiprisms.

Twisted body

The exemplary body on the right side is an arbitrary twisted body. In a twisted body, the lateral surfaces are deformed as well and form 4-sided saddle surfaces.

A twisted body is not an anti-prism. The lateral surface segments of an anti-prism are not flat. In a twisted body, the mantle surface segments are twisted in on themselves and usually form a multi-curved surface. It is intended to illustrate the difference between a twisted body and a twisted lateral surface.

basal surface

apical surface

Scutuid

A scutoid is a prism-like body. It has a curved surface and at least one vertex that does not lie on one of the two base surfaces.

Scutoids were first discovered in 2018 by a joint work by a team of biologists and mathematicians in Spain to describe and name them.

The starting point of this research group was the research into the 3-dimensional organisation of simple cell layers with a curved organ surfaces in multicellular animals

Within the framework of generative geometric developments, cell types could be anticipated and subsequently confirmed by investigations on the animal cells.

The geometry of the scutoid allows the packaging of four cells at only two anchor points. Thanks to its simple constructive design, shell shapes with different cells can be quickly developed and implemented.

The scutoid is, in the context of generative design, an example of how new objects with their own properties continue to be discovered, determined and quickly incorporated into design practice.

KNOWN VOLUMES

Tetrahedron

Hexahedron

Octahedron

Dodecahedron

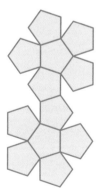

Icosahedron

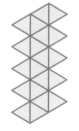

Platonic solids

The Platonic bodies are named after the
Greek philosopher Plato. They are 5 polyhedra
(polyhedra) with the greatest possible symmetry.
Each Platonic solid is bounded by several congruent regular polygons with the same congruence.
- tetrahedron, 4-sided
  consisting of 4 3-corners
- hexahedron, 6-surfaces
  consisting of 6 squares
- octahedron, 8-sided
  consisting of 8 equilateral 3-corners
- dodecahedron (pentagon dodecahedron),
  12-faces, consisting of 12 5-corners
- icosahedron, 20-sided
  consists of 20 3-corners

All Platonic solids are convex and in edges
of equal length meet in each corner. The faces
that meet are congruent. Therefore, none of the
corners can be distinguished from each other.

The body meshes shown on the left are only one
possible development, others are possible. Every
Platonic body is also suitable as a cube due to its
homogeneous weight distribution.

KNOWN VOLUMES

Truncated tetrahedron

Cuboctahedron

Hexahedron frustum

Octahedron frustum

Small
Rhombus-
cuboctahedron

Large
Rhombus-
cuboctahedron

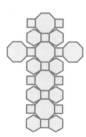

Bevelled
Hexahedron

Icosidodecahedron

Archimedean solids (1)

If one refers to the indistinguishability of faces and edges, which prevails in solids, one obtains Archimedean solids.

They are convex polyhedra with the following properties
– all side faces are regular polygons
– all corners are equal to each other
– they are not platonic solids, prisms or antiprisms.

There is disagreement about the number of Archimedean solids, depending on the way of counting there are either 13 of the 15 solids. These can be into the following groups
– tetrahedron group
– icosahedron group
– octahedron group

KNOWN VOLUMES

Dodecahedron frustum

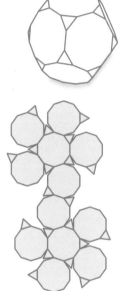

Truncated icosahedron
or football body

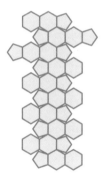

Rhombus-
icosidodecahedron

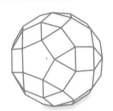
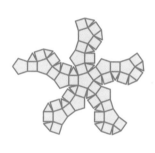

Great Rhombenicosidodecahedron
or truncated icosidodecahedron

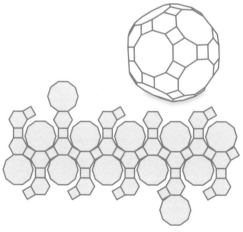

Bevelled
Dodecahedron

Archimedean solids (2)

When closely observing the structure of the
individual shell surfaces, it is noticeable that all
shell surfaces are developed with the same objects

△   –   equilateral 3-sided corner

▢   –   equilateral 4-corner (square)

⬡   –   equilateral 6-sided corner

⯃   –   equilateral 8-sided corner

⬣   –   equilateral 10-sided corner

On the one hand, the representation of the
mantle surface as a development serves a
better understanding of the respective body
and, on the other hand, clarifies the modular
structure not only of the individual bodies but
of all bodies.

In practice, these bodies often serve as a starting
point for further design studies.

Triakis traeder

Tetrakis hexahedron

Triakis octahedron

Triacis icosahedron

Hexakis octahedron

Pentakis dodecahedron

Hexakis icosahedron

Rhombus-
dodecahedron

Rhombus-
triacontahedron

Deltoid-
icositetrahedron

Deltoid-
hexacontahedron

Catalan solids

The 13 Catalan solids are named after the Belgian mathematician Eugéne Charles Catalan. Catalan solids are convex polyhedra.

Like the Platonic solids, the Catalan solids consist of congruent faces. That is why the illustrations on the left do not show folding patterns, but rather a congruent surface from which the respective body is derived.

The difference between Catalan solids and Platonic solids is that corners and edges can be different. With Platonic solids these are the same.

Pentagon-
ikositetraeder

Pentagon-
icositetrahedron

KNOWN VOLUMES

Dodecahedron star

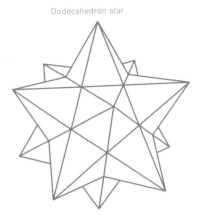

Icosahedron star

Great dodecahedron

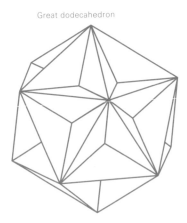

Great icosahedron

Kepler-Poinsot-solids

The Kelper-Poinsot bodies are stellar bodies, as their appearance suggests. They are regular, non-convex polyhedra. Johannes Kepler (1571-1630) discovered the dodecahedron star and the icosahedron star and Louis Poinsot (1777-1859) the two great dodecahedra.

Their shape derives from the abandonment of the condition of convexity in the Platonic solids.

The dodecahedron star consists of 60 equal isosceles 3-corners, which are all at the same dihedral angle of 116.57° to each other.

The icosahedron star consists of 60 equal isosceles 3-corners, the dihedral angles are 63.44°.

The great icosahedron consists of 60 isosceles and 120 irregular 3-corners.

KNOWN VOLUMES

Johnson solids (1)

In 1966 Norman Johnson published a list of 92 solids. These solids are an enumeration of all convex solids bounded only by regular polygons. The Johnson solids include neither Platonic and Archimedean solids, nor prisms and anti-prisms.

Common with the Catalan solids is that the corners of a Johnson solid are not identical. A special feature among the Johnson bodies is the pseudo-rhombic cuboctahedron (J37), whose corners are locally uniform but not globally.

In 1969, Wictor Salgaller confirmed the completeness of the list.

The surfaces of the Johnson solids consist of the regular faces shown below. For standardised representation, each edge length was determined with the value 1.

△ – equilateral 3-sided corner

▢ – equilateral 4-corner (square)

⬡ – equilateral 6-sided corner

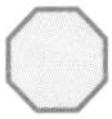

⯃ – equilateral 8-sided corner

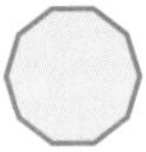

⬟ – equilateral 10-sided corner

KNOWN VOLUMES

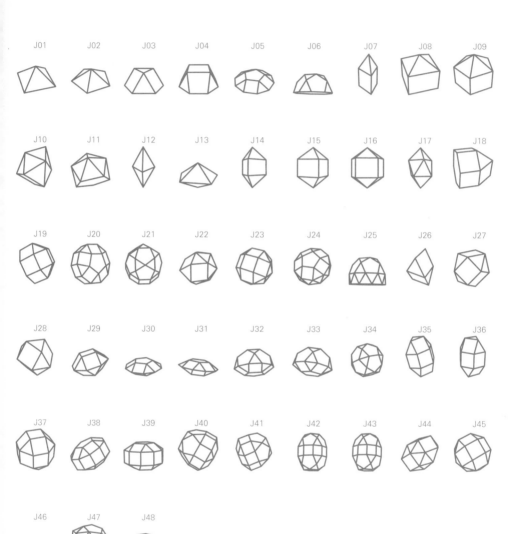

Johnson solids (2)

Pyramids, domes and rotundas
  J01. Quadrangle pyramid
  J02. Pentagonal pyramid
  J03. Triangular dome
  J04. Square dome
  J05. Pentagonal dome
  J06. Pentagonal rotunda

Modified pyramids
  J07. Elongated 3-corner pyramid
  J08. Extended square pyramid
  J09. Extended 5-corner pyramid
  J10. Twisted extended square pyramid
  J11. Twisted extended 5-corner pyramid
  J12. 3-corner bi-pyramid
  J13. Pentagonal bipyramid
  J14. Elongated triangular bipyramid
  J15. Extended square bipyramid
  J16. Elongated pentagonal bipyramid
  J17. Twisted extended square bipyramid

Modified domes and rotundas
  J18. Extended triangular dome
  J19. Extended square dome
  J20. Elongated pentagonal dome
  J21. Extended pentagonal rotunda
  J22. Twisted elongated triangular dome
  J23. Twisted extended square dome
  J24. Twisted extended pentagonal dome
  J25. Twisted extended pentagonal rotunda
  J26. Twisted double wedge
  J27. Triangular double dome
  J28. Square double dome
  J29. Twisted square double dome
  J30. Pentagonal double dome
  J31. Twisted pentagonal double dome
  J32. Pentagonal dome rotunda
  J33. Twisted pentagonal dome rotunda

  J34. Pentagonal double rotunda
  J35. Extended triangular double dome
  J36. Extended twisted triangular double dome
  J37. Extended twisted square double dome
  J38. Extended pentagonal double dome
  J39. Extended twisted pentagonal double dome
  J40. Extended pentagonal dome rotunda
  J41. Extended twisted pentagonal dome rotunda
  J42. Extended pentagonal double rotunda
  J43. Extended twisted pentagonal double rotunda
  J44. Twisted extended triangular double dome
  J45. Twisted extended square double dome
  J46. Twisted extended pentagonal double dome
  J47. Twisted extended pentagonal dome rotunda
  J48. Twisted extended pentagonal double rotunda

KNOWN VOLUMES

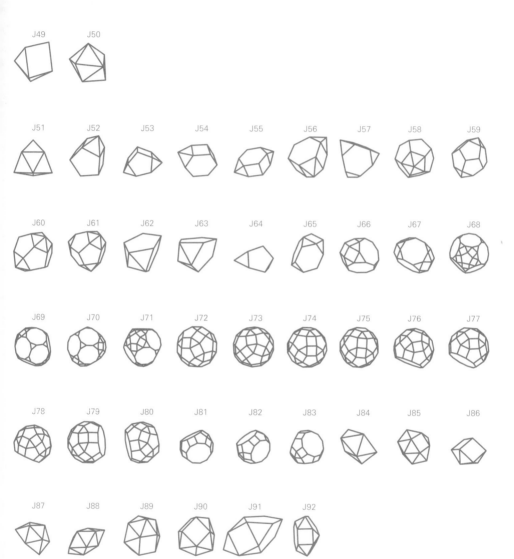

Johnson solids (3)

Extended prisms

J49. Extended triangular prism
J50. Double enlarged triangular prism
J51. Triple extended triangular prism
J52. Extended pentagonal prism
J53. Double extended pentagonal prism
J54. Extended hexagon prism
J55. Double extended hexagon prism para
J56. Double extended hexagon prism meta
J57. Triple extended hexagon prism

Modified platonic solids

J58. Extended dodecahedron
J59. Doubly extended dodecahedron (para)
J60. Doubly expanded dodecahedron (meta)
J61. Triple expanded dodecahedron
J62. Double truncated icosahedron (meta)
J63. Triple truncated icosahedron
J64. Expanded triple truncated icosahedron

Modified Archimedean solids

J65. Expanded truncated tetrahedron
J66. Expanded truncated hexahedron
J67. Double expanded truncated hexahedron
J68. Expanded truncated dodecahedron
J69. Double extended truncated dodecahedron (para)
J70. Doubly expanded truncated dodecahedron (meta)
J71. Triple extended truncated dodecahedron
J72. Twisted rhombicosidodecahedron
J73. Double twisted small rhombenicosidodecahedron (para)
J74. Double twisted small rhombenicosidodecahedron (meta)
J75. Triple twisted small rhombenicosidodecahedron
J76. Truncated small rhombenicosidodecahedron
J77. Twisted truncated small rhombenicosidodecahedron (para)
J78. Twisted truncated small rhombenicosidodecahedron (meta)
J79. Double twisted truncated small rhombenicosidodecahedron
J80. Double truncated small rhombenicosidodecahedron (para)
J81. Double truncated small rhombenicosidodecahedron (meta)
J82. Twisted double truncated small rhombenicosidodecahedron
J83. Triple truncated small rhombenicosidodecahedron

Other

J84. Trigondodecahedron
J85. Bevelled square antiprism
J86. Sphenocorona
J87. Extended sphenocorona
J88. Sphenomegacorona
J89. Lifting sphenomegacorona
J90. Disphenocingulum
J91. Biluna double rotunda
J92. Triangular hebespheno rotunda

"Man is the measure of all things"

The Homo Mensura theorem is attributed to the Greek philosopher Protagoras

There area no limits to the possibilities,
operations have no limits. Be it in the
development of new operations or in the
combination of different operations.

Shaping operations can be subdivided into:
- technical
- narrative

Technical operations are the
- modelling
  for spline bodies (mechanical)
- transforming
  for geometric bodies (mathematical)

Narrative operations are
- figurative associative
- forming characters
- forming "stories
- statement forming
- concept clarifying
- etc.

Technical

Modelling comes from a mathematical understanding of shaping.

2 dimensional

Objects that are modulated are understood as autonomous volumes or surfaces. The objects consist of a network of splines, which determine the surface of the object.

- points determine the height, low and points of the contours and the volumes.
- vectors control the contour the course of the surface.
- the mesh can also be described as a "skin".

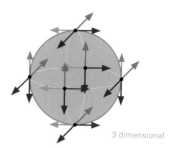

3 dimensional

Narrative

In narrative, everything from the figurative to the conceptual can be told. In the development of a narrative operation, it is important to consider the viewer, because if the viewer does not recognise the narrative, the object "loses" its narrative power.

In the following, the mechanical formative operations are dealt with. All operations are valid in 2-dimensional and 3-dimensional space.

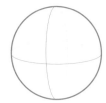

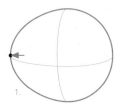

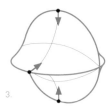

Modelling

Volumes that are modelled are determined by their closed surface. The surface consists of a mesh. This mesh has points that are provided with vectors. This results in three possible changeable parameters

1. the position of a point
2. the strength of a vector
3. the direction of a vector

For the volume development by means of points and vectors are

- curved surfaces
- the edge development

are of particular interest.

Volumes that can be developed from standard solids are dealt with in the chapter Transformation. Modelling does not exclude transformative operations.

Transforming

Transformative operations come
from a mechanical understanding.

To make it easier to understand, the structure
of all the following operations was considered
as a positive surface, volume or space. Internal
surfaces and negative volumes are not taken into
account in the following considerations, but they
represent an equal tool in the transformation of
objects.

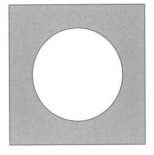

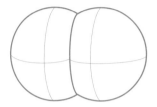

Add

The word comes from the latin word additio, addere (to add). An addition of bodies only makes sense if at least two bodies penetrate each other. otherwise, the designer can continue to consider the two individual bodies separately.

Only surfaces can be added to surfaces and only bodies can be added to bodies. In an addition, one considers the subsequent object as the product of the operation. This product, in turn, can be used as an object for further shaping operations.

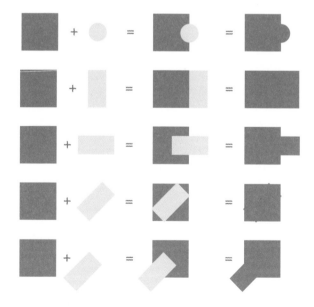

Subtract

The word "subtraction" comes from the latin (subtrahere) and means as much as "to pull away", "to remove". To do this, at least two objects must penetrate each other; either only areas or only volumes can be subtracted from each other.

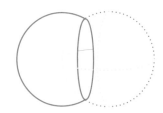

In a subtraction, one object is determined from which the intersection is subtracted and one object is determined as the intersection object. Layers and shapes are freely selectable as long as they form an intersection.

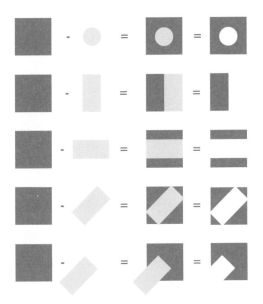

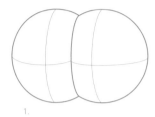

1.

2.

3.

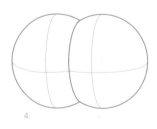

4.

Boolean operation

The Boolean operation is named after George Boole. Boole defined 16 Boolean operations (see below). He describes operations in software development and they find application in queries, among other things. For the designer, four of these operations are important when dealing with two bodies (see left).

1. adding the two solids
2. subtracting the intersection of one body
3. forming the intersection of two bodies
4. forming the non-intersection of two bodies Solids

Only surfaces with surfaces and only solids with solids can be processed. With three objects the other 12 operations are used, The diagram below presents all possible combinations.

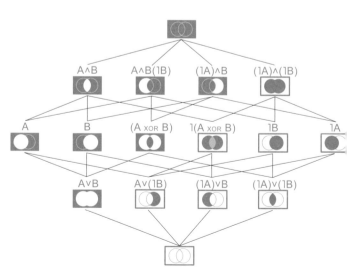

Scaling

Compression is understood as a change in length under pressure. The circumscribed area or volume of the object increases or decreases. Scaling is a uniform change in the size of an object:
1. increase
2. reduce

Non-uniform scaling is:
3. compress
4. stretch

Components of an object can also be be scaled:
5. contour thickness

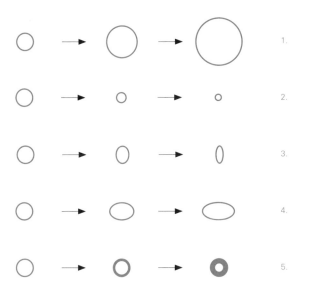

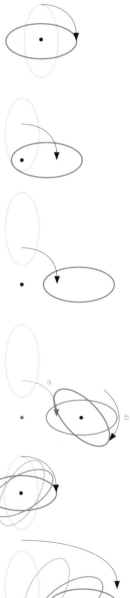

Rotate

Rotation means turning an object around at least one axis. This changes the position and the direction of the object.

The point around which the object is rotated can be positioned in different ways in relation to the rotated object:

1. in the centre of the object
2. at any point within the object
3. at any point outside the object
4. several different rotations can be superimposed
5. the rotation can be divided into any steps
6. the point at which the rotation takes place is moving during the rotation. In the example the displacement takes place along the contour of a line. Both movements are overlaping.

114

Turning surfaces

For the rotation of a spline, the rotation axis around which the spline is rotated is determined.

The rotation axis can:
1. lie in the centre of the object
2. be at the edge of the object
3. be outside the object at any position
4. the rotation can be divided into arbitrary steps
5. several different rotations can be used at the same time

The spline itself can also be arbitrarily shaped
1. open
2. pointed
3. closed
4. concave
5. convex

Resulting bodies of revolution whose cross-sections intersect during rotation are disregarded. Of course, different operations can be applied to the surfaces of rotation at the same time.

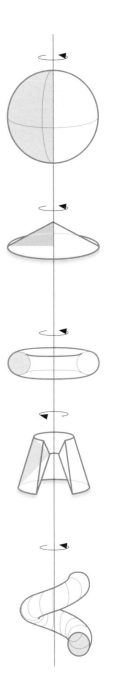

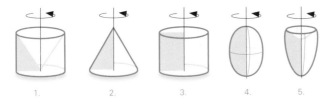

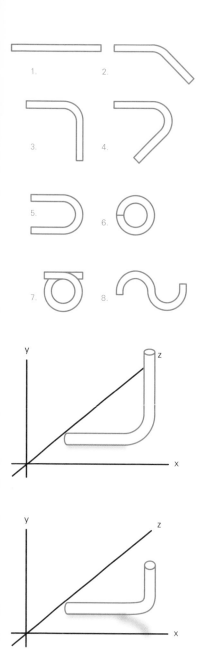

Bending

When bending, the direction of a shape is changed. In the process, the volume of the shape is maintained. Mechanically, when bending, the surface of the outer bending radius is stretched and that of the inner radius is compressed. This is of no importance in formal design.

A bend can take any direction, the developed bend is most simply determined by the bending radius and the bending angle. There are

1. straight
2. obtuse bends
3. right-angled bend
4. acute bend
5. reversing bends
6. closed bends
7. continuing bend, loop
8. multiple bends

To determine the bend, a reference plane is created, because a bend can be created freely in 3-dimensional space.

8. bend is congruent with an existing plane
9. bend is freely created in space

116

Wrapping

When wrapping, one or more objects are arranged as desired and provided with a contour or shell. This contour can be subject to arbitrary rules of its own.

1. incomplete wrapping
2. minimum surface
3. multiple sheathing
4. shortest connection
5. simplifying sheathing
6. forking

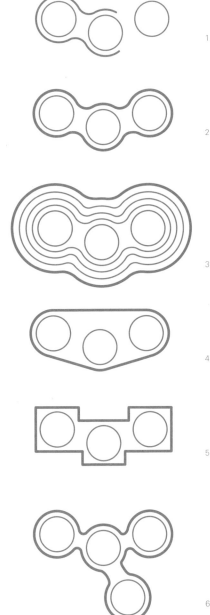

Symmetry

Symmetry comes from the Greek and means as much as "uniformity" or "evenness". Today, symmetry is understood as an arrangement and relationship tool with which an object is mirrored, rotated or shifted over a point or an axis.

1. axial symmetry
2. displacement symmetry
3. point symmetry
4. rotational symmetry

Mirror

An object is mirrored on a mirror axis. For the mirrored body, this means that it cannot be identical to the first object, but has been "flipped" from "left to right": ❰ ❱

The mirror axis can
1. intersect the object
2. lie outside the object
3. be positioned freely in space
4. distort the mirrored object
5. create several reflections
6. reproduce sections

Projection

Any contour is projected onto any object.
The contour can be projected in different ways:

1. as a whole
2. as a section
3. enlarging
4. reducing
5. distorting

Depending on the course of the projection
surface, the projected result can be deformed
again.

The combination of projection and subsequent
mirroring onto another surface creates unimagin-
able and highly complex contours and shapes that
can only be developed in practice or in appropriate
animation programmes.

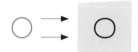

1.

2.

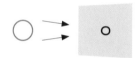

3.

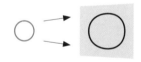

4.

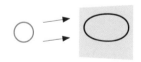

5.

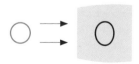

6.

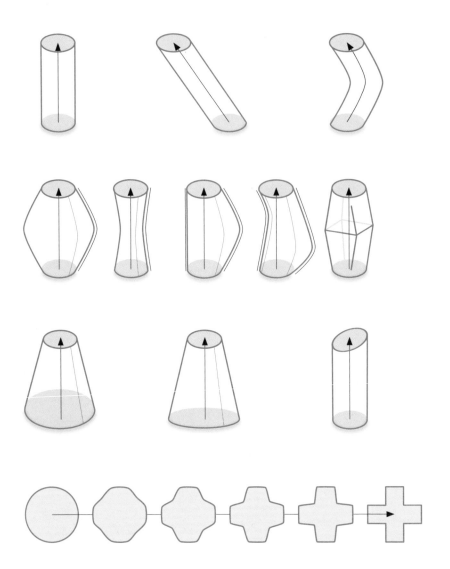

Morphological transitions

A morphological transition in space consists of
at least
- two cross-sections (the base surface
  and the top surface)
- a lateral surface,

which develops a homogeneous transition
between the two cross-sections. The shell surface
can be additionally controlled and manipulated
with paths.

Design parameters are
- the position of the base and top surfaces
  in relation to each other
- the shape of the cross-sections
- the number of cross-sections
- the type of morphological transitions

They can be combined with each other in any way.

Morphological transitions in the plane are divided
into stages.

It is subdivided into
- start and target object
- intermediate steps

The number of intermediate steps can be arbitrarily
large, there should be at least 2 in order to clearly
represent the morphological transition.

ARRANGING OPERATIONS

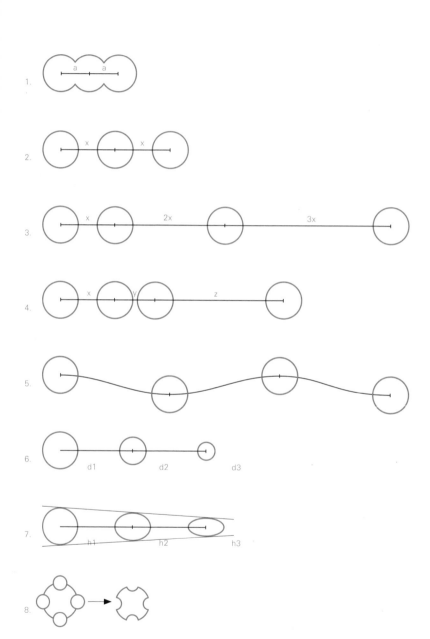

1.

2.

3.

4.

5.

6.

7.

8.

Arrangement:
- sequence (one line)

Sequences belong to the field of packings, where individual bodies are related to each other by means of their position.

In a ries, the same body can appear several times in the repetition: ▌ ▌

The ordering has three possible results.
1. a new body is created, comparable to an addition or a Boolean operation.
2. a group is created from individual bodies

The ranking can be carried out in different ways:
2. linear with regular spacing
3. linear with regular changing distances
4. linear with irregular distances
5. following a curve

The sequence can be combined with other shaping operations, e.g.
6. scale
7. compress
8. subtract

Series can also have different directions and be combined with different transforming and modelling operations (8.).

ARRANGING OPERATIONS

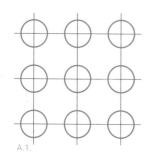

A.1.

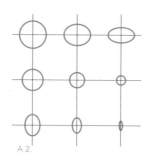

A.2.

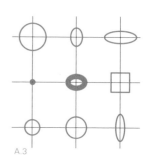

A.3

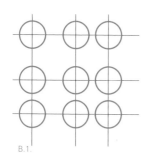

B.1.

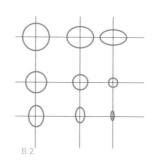

B.2.

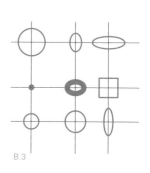

B.3

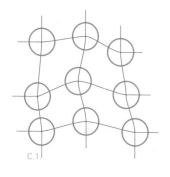

C.1.

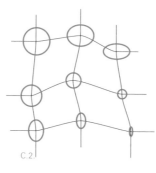

C.2.

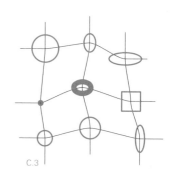

C.3

Arrangement:
- – net (sequence in two directions)
- – grid (sequence in three directions)

In a net and in a grid
- – a layout
- – an object
- – an operation

are combinable with each other.
Each of the elements of a net can be
- – uniform
- – regular
- – irregular

The example of the net is used to
present the different combinations.
On the x-axis:
- A. uniform net
- B. regular net
- C. irregular net

On the Y-axis:
1. uniform object
2. regular object
3. irregular object

For grids, the same procedure and division apply as for the mesh, with the difference that for
the grid the depth (Z-axis) is added to the length
(Y-axis) and width (X-axis).

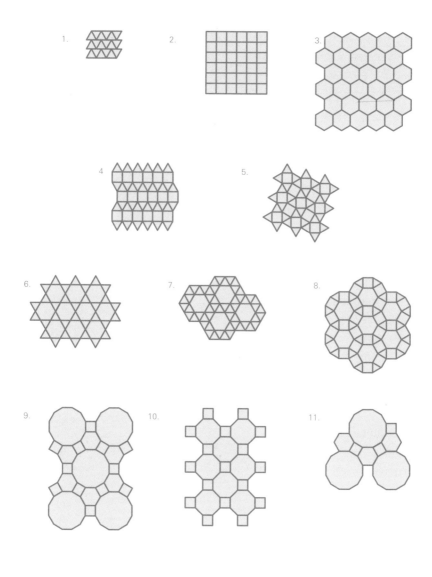

Arrangement:
- Parquetry, tiling, paving, surface closure

Parquetry is a separate and very broad field
and will only be hinted at here in its basic form.

This ensures the
- gapless and
- overlap-free
covering of a
- flat plane
- 3d plane
- volume
by uniform parts.

Platonic or regular parquetry
1. triangle; 2. square; 3. 6-corner

Archimedean, semi-regular or 1-uniform parking
4. 3-3-3-4-4; 5. 3-3-4-3-4; 6. 3-6-3-6; 7. 3-3-3-3-6
8. 3-4-6-4; 9. 3-12-12; 10. 4-8-8; 11. 4.6.12

For your own studies,
the following keywords are helpful for research:
- symmetries in parquetry
- scarcity technique
- aperiodic parquetry
- apollonian nets (Apollonius of Perge)
- penrose parquetries
- regular, demiregular, irregular polygons
- isohedral and anisohedral
- aperiodic

Transver
The transver is a conceptual design tool.

In order to consider the transver design method, its siblings must also be considered:

- Inspiration
  In word usage, inspiration is not an active designing: "one is inspired". One of the muses kisses one and after that one follows this inspiration. It seems like inspiration might be a passive design tool.
- Quote
  In a quotation, a designer refers one or more previous works. In doing so, the new work becomes an homage, a critical or an ironic analysis or a commentary. Here are
- Plagiarism
  Plagiarism is the simple copying of an idea, concept or form.

Transver stands between inspiration, quotation and plagiarism. It differs in that the designer has gained knowledge through observation and modulates this knowledge to fit his or her own conception. The knowledge gained can be of a formal or conceptual nature.

Designers who work methodically use the module "research" in their projects. In this way, designers expose themselves in a planned way to the knowledge gained from previous work. The motivation for research varies greatly,

- own lack of ideas
- protection against parallel developments
- grasping current zeitgeist
- start for further idea or concept development

These insights influence one`s own design work both positively and negatively. The flowing boundaries between these siblings quickly become clear.

In the ideal case, the designer picks up from one thematic area

- a technique
- a material or
- a formal language

and gives it a new meaning in another field, adapting its knowledge to the new requirements and thereby creating a transver which at the same time represents an innovation.

"Design is Relative"
The recognition of design quality depends on time, space and the viewer.

What is "design"?

Companies from different sectors (mechanical engineering, consumer goodas, software development, finance, fashion, etc.) are currently publishing job advertisements for designers.

The fact that the job descriptions contradict each other in terms of content and the required education does not seem to bother anyone. Be it the job description, the field of activity, the training or the salary. In the industry there is obviously no common understanding of what a designer is and what a designer does. Even within a design agency with graphic, product, interaction, service UI and UX designers, the term is explained and lived differently. This clearly shows the current problems of the design profession - there seems to have been a dilution of terminology and previous descriptions are no longer reflected in practice.

"Design" is not understood and used in the same way everywhere. Terms like "Gestaltung" or "Design" stand for "creative" work, as far as everyone seems to agree. In the process, the problem of explanation is linguistically shifted from "design" to "creative", which is thus not a practicable explanation.

The question "what is design?"
is followed by other questions:
- What is a designer?
- How does one recognise design?
- What is a design process?
- What are designed products?

The aim of the chapter is,
- to explain what design is and what design can do,
- to introduce interdisciplinary design methods
- to create a comprehensible basis for dialogue
  for the different design disciplines.

And finaly
- What makes design to a good design?

What is the cook's recipe, ...

A chef has a limited number of different raw materials at his disposal, which he can prepare using a limited number of different processing methods.

Cooks specialise in depth not breadth.
By this he creates his own unique signature style.
- e.g. preparing fish in as many different ways as possible,
- to prepare as much as possible in a wok,
- to prepare only desserts,
- rediscovering long-forgotten recipes
- and so on and so forth.

In addition, the chef sees the result of his work as a holistic customer experience. This also includes the ambience in which the food is served, from the reservation to the napkin to the lighting. The chef controls the context in which the experience takes place.

In order for the guests to have a comparable experience, the chef uses a recipe to determine how, what and when is to be prepared and presented.
Generally speaking, the recipe defines the connections
- the relationships between the ingredients
- and their preparation method,
- the surrounding where and how it will presented
thus influences the user experience as imagined by the chef.
Recipes are used in two ways:
- in development, it serves as a tool in which the relationships of the individual ingredients or preparation types are developed and optimised.
- in implementation, a recipe describes the reproducible production path.

... are the designer`s models and technical drawings.

Like the chef, the designer also has a limited selection
of materials and production methods at his disposal.
The designer also creates new things by combining them.

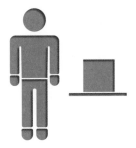

Designers also specialise in certain themes
- be it their own handwriting
- a certain product area
- a certain manufacturing or production process
- a certain company
- and many other possible themes

Ideas are presented on the basis of sketches, while
relationships between individual components are
developed and checked. Proportions are determined,
materials and manufacturing processes are predefined.
Individual connections are checked for their holistic
expression.

The designer develops an emotional expression by combining
- materials
- function
- the way of using it
- application
- manufacturing process

To check the developed relationships, the designer creates
samples, models and technical drawings.

Samples, models and technical drawings are used in two ways:
- in development to check and refine details
- in the implementation as a template for the design

**The comparison of "cook and designer"
shows structural relatives.**

Both
- work with limiting factors,
  which they constantly recombine
- new raw materials are rarely found
  or new processes are developed
- know their target group and strive to offer them
  a desirable experience
- realise visions by planning the identification, development
  and recognising, developing and balancing all the
  necessary perfecting, all necessary interrelationships
- combine known raw materials and production processes
  into new experiences
- document the development process and the result in
  a recipe or a technical drawing.
- use work instructions for the more advanced trades
- work with a claim to innovation

The external restrictions and the focus on one customer or user
are clearly recognisable. The creative process is characterised
by combining existing individual factors and anticipating how
the intended target group will react to them. In addition, it is
important to consider how the result of the design work can be
reproduced again and again.

The designer is characterised by the levelling development of
combinations, i.e. the deliberate and purposeful interrelations-
hip. This form of combination can be called composition.

The comparison between cook and designer shows that
- the development of relationships
- the balancing of contexts
- relating the product to its environment
- predicting how the user will react to it
- determining how the result should be

are the universal activities of every designer. This view allows for a common understanding of what "design" is across disciplines.

This statement is not only valid for the design process, but also for the reading and interpretation of a designed work. The intention of the developed network of relationships can be checked as an effect on the user. If the user of the new product acts as the designer planned in advance, it will be a successful product. The product is an optimal result if it has become a sought-after product in the target group

To achieve this goal, the various design disciplines use a wide variety of tools, each of which requires its own specialisation in training. However, the methods and the intention are the common features of all design professions.

The consequence of these observations is that a designed product should only be evaluated in the context of its intention and its effect (on its target group).

For good reason, because the quality of shape-giving operations depends on the context in which they are used. They do not have universal correctness. What turns out to be the right form development in one situation may turn out to be wrong in another context.

What is design?

The difference between making forms and giving form lies
in the complexity, the consideration of the many different
requirements and the necessary methodical approach.
- methodical procedure
- the planning and creation
innovations, which makes a form maker into a designer.
Tools and methods, some of which are presented in this book,
are necessary.

Generally speaking, this means that:
Design is
- the intentional process of determining form.
- not to assign a function or application to a
found form.

Products are designed when they
- are the result of solution-oriented thinking.

Designers are:
- People who methodically develop and apply
formgiving processes.

It is the "how" that distinguishes making from designing.

Successful implementation of a design process

The following basic steps are part of a successful design process:
0. A task or problem is identified and formulated.
1. The designer asks "why".
   The necessity of a possible solution is examined.
2. The designer reformulates the task as an open question. (e.g. "How can ...?").
3. The designer answers the question from point 2. with as many different answers as possible.
4. The designer selects further ideas, and develops in-depth questions on the requirements of the product.
5. The designer develops the selected idea into a visible/ perceptible form.
6. Step 5 is repeated as a loop until the level of detail is sufficient.
7. The solution is presented in the form of sketches and models.
8. Is the task or problem really solved?
   Have no new problems been developed?
   If yes, in worst case go to point 1.
9. Implementation

Can anyone do it?
The design process described above thrives on the following skills
1. being able to take ownership of the task at hand,
2. the empathic ability to put oneself in the future user,
3. asking the "right" questions,
4. to recognise the best answers by means of criteria,
5. to be able to decide on a compromise,
6. to formulate and present all answers comprehensibly
7. not to be satisfied.

In order to better understand the nature of design, the term intelligence is briefly examined. Describing the term intelligence from the point of view of design, one obtains a useful understanding of design. Intelligence consists of four building blocks:

- the striving to discover connections and to developing
- evaluating the quality of the new contexts
- learning the contexts and their quality
- how and whether the learned knowledge is used.

This means that the designer needs a minimum of intelligence in order to always discover and develop connections. This form of intelligence can and is trained within the framework of a university education.

This description of intelligence shows the interface with the user, because the user is also constantly striving to create, find and interpret connections. For the designer, this behavioural pattern is the most important thing about human beings. Every human being constantly observes and interprets his environment, e.g. he relates a dead tree branch to a rising wind. This turns the branch into a potential danger for the human being, or he sees the burning value of the branch and now recognises the useful firewood in the branch.

Perceived things are constantly compared with experienced, learned and instinctive knowledge. Always with the intention of using recognised relationships

- to develop even more reliable prognoses
- to obtain even better orientation.

What is acquired, innate or self-experienced is not a question that the designer can answer. The designer accepts this behavioural pattern and uses it sensibly for his work.

The example of the branch makes it clear that there is no such thing as a "good branch". Only the context from which a person observes an object makes an evaluation possible. The value of the branch is determined by the context that a person makes within his observation. More generally, this means,
  – good design is relative.
Because a well-designed product depends on the context in which the observer places it.

How can we understand the work of a designer?

The designer examines and creates networks of relationships. He checks these for their effect, discards "bad" ones and refines "better" ones. The better the developed network of relationships is adapted to the needs of the user and the user can also use them, the easier it is for the target group to get involved and to value the product. The more attractive the network of relationships is, the more desirable the product is.

Models, sketches and other representations allow the perception or non-perception of relationships to be checked. This allows the designer to match intention and effect. The user's later dialogue with the product is anticipated and intentionally controlled by the designer (e.g. "Where is the warning light?").

This is not to be confused with manipulation, but it is taking into account the abilities and possibilities of the user and thus supporting him in his intention. The better the user uses the product, the more successful the product is.

What is the use of this view?

If the designer understands the quality of his work as possibilities and dependencies on framework conditions
- he can orient his working method accordingly
- explain, compare and argue the intermediate steps of his work and argue
- evaluate results "objectively"

In practice, this means that the evaluation of a work can only take place in dependence of the context in which the product is located and cannot be done arbitrarily. This also means that a design solution is not arbitrarily transferable. What is an optimal solution in one task may be counterproductive in the next. The designer checks this by means of models, sketches and other methods of representation. If the context is similar, related results can be produced.

In the younger design disciplines, context is also part of the design work. On the basis of detailed user and product analyses, own scenarios are developed. In doing so, potential needs and behaviour patterns are anticipated and the corresponding products are designed.

The context is the sum of all relationships in which a product stands. A relationship is the connection between at least two variables.

The list of variables developed on the following pages does not claim to be complete. Designers are called upon to constantly re-sort and independently expand this list. The variables are evaluated in relation to the project and are always put in relation to each other. This should make it clear:

- how timeless and fashion-independent this understanding of design is,
- why there are and will be different forms of design and will continue to exist

Variables gain or lose importance over time, others are added. The significance of individual variables changes through the observer's point of view.

In one design, a variable can be the most important building block, in the next it plays no role. Even within a design process, the perspective changes and with it the meanings of individual variables. Designers are intuitively familiar with this approach.

Le Corbusier`s Modulor works according to a similar principle. The Modulor is not a static chain of numbers! In the Modulor, the body dimensions are in relation to furniture, rooms and buildings. If the body dimensions change, the furniture, the rooms and the buildings change. The relationships remain the same, the value of the variables changes - like in a mathematical equation. Le Corbusier has much emphasis on explaining the rules on which his proportions, expressed by his own metre-measurement and his own tables. In this way, the Modulor can always be adapted to the current proportions of the human being. Mind you, the context is not a modulator. Context is a bridge of understanding between the different design disciplines so that they can work together on joint projects in the future.

Once again briefly reminded listed:

Design is
- the form giving process of development,
- the intentional developing, composing and combination of relationships.

The following sentences are derived from this:
- Designed products are the results of this process.
- Designed products are works in which relationships have been and methodically dealt with relationships.

Designers are people,
- who define relationships within a product,
- anticipate the relationships of a product to its environment.

The cross check

Imagine a world consisting of randomness, disorder and, at worst, chaos. For some people, this is the world we live in. However, it is unbearable for us humans to live permanently in this idea.

Instead, people search for and create connections, always with the aim of orienting themselves and understanding their environment. Our curiosity is an expression of this quest for orientation.

That is why people find it difficult
- to believe in no divine authority,
- to give up their search for the world formula,
- to see no causality in their actions.

People find it difficult to accept the existence of chance alone. People would rather develop a plausible connection (in their understanding) between several events or objects than accept something as groundless.

Developing relationships, discovering relationships gives people a sense of security. By means of the constant development and adjustment of relationships, people orient themselves in their environment.

Which contexts people consider important and right is a constant social discourse and the designer is a responsible part of this society and this discourse.

Designers who accept this behaviour and work with it are able to create products that have a social meaning and that the user will find desirable.

How can relationships be developed methodically?

Questions build relationships.
1. why
    a. Why should the product exist?
2. what
    a. What is it supposed to do?
    b. What should it be able to do?
    c. What should I do with it?
3. where
    a. Where will it be located?
    b. Where will it be optimally used?
    c. Where will it be stowed?
4. how
    a. How is it made?
    b. How is it used?
    c. How is it disposed of?
5. who
    a. Who should manufacture it?
    b. Who is to use it?

These and other questions are considered and answered by the designer in the design. All questions, except the why-question, can be answered simply, quickly and precisely. The why question is the first and most important question. It asks for the reason of a product. With the answer to the why question, all other questions become very easy to answer.

Users who percept the dialogue of questioning and asking in the product automatically establish there own dialogical based relationship with the product. In the process, users are developing there own questions and answers.

This arouses the user's sympathy for the product.
He will value the product. The designer is able to trigger
this often unconscious dialogue with the user by means of
his design in a way that is appropriate for the target group.

To give the designer an overview of the important criteria in
his project, he develops project specific evaluation criteria in
the form of a matrix, a grid.

A matrix is an evaluation canon or filter. It is not static and can
be modified in the course of a project. The matrix reflects the
current state of knowledge of a designer.

Thanks to the grid, the designer is able to keep an overview,
to formulate his work transparently, to question it during implementation and to optimise it. The grid is a tool with which
the designer can systematically introduce new findings into the
project. He can explain the differences between variants and
develop further variants. He thus finds himself in a methodical
design process. In which he develops dependencies, describes
them and optimises their readability.

Designers tend to start the actual creative work as late as
possible and push other work ahead. The documentary preparation of a grid is only worthwhile for large or complex projects.
Manageable projects only need tuning on the soundtrack.

It makes sense to agree on a rough network of relationships
with the design team before starting a project. The network
of relationships is spun more and more tightly in the course
of the project in order to formulate more precise requirements
for the detailed elaboration.

Which variables can the designer relate?

1. within the product
   a. areas
   b. edges
   c. course of surfaces
   d. edge course
   e. volume
   f. components and assemblies
   g. proportions
2. formal
   a. material
   b. shape
   c. texture
   d. position/location
   e. haptics
   f. weight
3. product to product
   a. product to product predecessor
   b. modularity within a series/product group
   c. to products of competitors
   d. interfaces, connections
4. product to man
   a. the user
   b. the observer
      (people define others via products, who use them)
   c. target group affiliation
5. product to the environment
   a. in development
   b. in use, under special conditions of use
   c. in disposal
6. product to culture
   a. history (time)
   b. art

c. technology
d. literature
e. music
f. politics
g. society

What is being designed?

A designer creates products, systems and structures, scenarios, patterns of use, patterns of behaviour, affiliations to social groups.

1. graphics
    a. typography
    b. product graphics
    c. print media (book/magazine/poster/flyer ...)
    d. information and guidance systems
       (orientation systems, instructions for use)
2. products (commodities)
    A. consumer goods
        a. white goods
        b. brown goods
        c. fashion
        d. electronics
    B. industrial products
        a. production lines
        b. production machines
        c. finishing machines
3. human-machine interaction
    A. operation 2D (Graphic User Interfaces)
        a. user icons
        b. user interfaces
        c. behavioural options (gestures/movements)
        d. action possibilities (application logics)

      B. operation 3D
         a. control and operating elements
           (buttons/handlebars/handles...)
         c. control units (control panel, devices...)
         d. behavioural patterns/movement sequences
         e. possible actions
    4. machine-machine interaction
         a. work process sequences
         b. communication processes/protocols/
           monitoring/forecasting
    5. man himself
      A. embellishment
         a. cosmetics
         b. hairstyle
         c. tattoo
      B. alterations
         a. cosmetic surgery
         b. bodybuilding
      C. fashion
         a. textile
         b. cut
         c. jewellery
    6. processes/procedures
         a. shaping operations
         b. functional series
         c. operations in work processes
         d. organisation charts
    ...

This list cannot possibly be complete. Basically, it can
be said that design takes place wherever relationships are
systematically developed and people are offered orientation.

Relationships serve positioning and orientation

The designer's task is to use this human behaviour for the user.
He offers the user positioning and orientation in different ways.

Positioning If man wants to orient himself, he must first determine
his point of view. To do this, he relates himself to his environment.
The designer supports the user by understanding the factors that
determine the position as variables.

1. space (where am I?)
2. time (when am I?)
3. direction (where do I come from? Where do I want to go?)
4. social/societal
    a. income
    b. status
    c. group membership
    d. attitude
    e. faith

Orientation If the person knows his position,
he can give himself direction on the following points:

1. purchase decision
2. use
3. maintenance
4. further use
4. disposal (of the product)

Humans are constantly looking for new contexts.

Man is constantly combining everything (anew). This is what is meant by curiosity. Curiosity is the search for and finding of relationships. Man relates everything, everyone and everything to each other.

Man implements this behaviour in different ways:
1. playfully
2. haphazardly
3. structured
4. methodically
5. culturally
6. sensory
7. sequence (chronological, hierarchical, numerical, spatial...)
8. empirical

This is true in the design process as well as in the perception of a product.

Creating connections that others can recognise is a job that requires a lot of empathy. The designer has to take a big step back again and again, pretending to see his work for the first time. In the process, the designer observes himself as he discovers the "new" product. Insights from this approach lead to a realignment of the web of relationships or a readjustment of variables.

Intention and effect are two sides of the same coin.

For the designer and for the user, relationships
are only a means to an end.

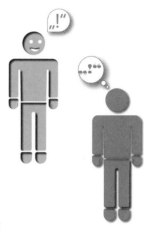

On the one hand, there is the designer who develops
relationships. He wants to express an idea or an issue by
means of a composition and combination of relationships.
On the other hand, there is the user who is looking for
relationships in order to be able to orientate himself.

The user can find beauty in the designer's composition,
perceive it as aesthetically pleasing. However, this is rarely
the sole criterion for the success of a product.

Only when the designer knows the framework conditions,
1. users
   a. with which senses (incl. their limitations)
      does the user perceive the product
   b. what is the cultural and social background
      of the user (target group)?
2. environmental conditions
   a. area of use
   b. environmental conditions
he can design a target group optimised product.

The user chooses a product that promises him the best possible positioning and orientation. However, the user rarely selects a product according to a single criterion. As a rule, they weigh up various aspects and look for the best personal compromise. The catalogue of requirements on which the user bases his or her purchase decision sometimes contains contradictory criteria and the relationships between the individual requirements are dynamic. According to which criteria does a purchase decision take place:

1. sensory:
    a. smell
    b. tasting
    c. hearing
    d. touch
    e. sight
2. emotional:
    a. love
    b. recognition
    c. fear
    d. disappointment
    e. belief
    f. moral value system (e.g. Fairtrade)
    g. humour
    h. brand image
    i. history
3. rational (objectively measurable parameters)
    a. functionality
    b. weight
    c. price
4. pseudorational (seemingly rational reasons)
    a. e.g. "particularly large boot...".
5. curiosity (the desire for variety)
    a. fashion

6. personality (Inner view of one's own person)
    a. identification
    b. personal preferences
    c. expression of one's own attitude to life
    d. fashion
7. status (Desired external perception of one's own person)
    a. social statement
    b. group affiliation
    c. social affiliation
    d. fashion
    e. wanting to be an innovator (an avant-gardist, in the literal sense)
8. promotion/support
    a. grants from third parties
    b. user purchases
9. price
    a. particularly low/high
    b. corresponds to the estimated budget
10. trust
    a. in the appearance of the product
    b. in the brand
    c. in the dealer
    d. in the advice of a friend or professional
11. sympathy
    a. for the brand
    b. for the dealer
    c. towards the product
12. reduce to key criteria
    a. e.g. particularly light
13. area of application
    a. outdoor
    b. semi-public space
    c. indoor

14. quality
    a. durability
    b. repairability
    c. maintenance intensity
15. livecycle
    a. raw material procurement
    b. working conditions in manufacturing
    c. transport conditions
    d. disposal
16. financing
    a. exchange
    b. rent
    c. lease
    d. buy

The above incomplete list shows how many criteria lead to a purchase decision and thus a compromise is unavoidable. In addition, the user is usually exposed to further external criteria:

1. functionality
    a. ease of use
    b. ergonomic
    c. more user-friendly
    d. extended functionalities
    e. specialised functionalities
2. brand
    a. status
    b. quality promise
    c. identification
3. aesthetics
    a. understanding of values
    b. cultural reference
4. costs
    a. in acquisition
    b. in maintenance
    c. in disposal

5. time
   a. finding the product in the market
   b. availability
   c. learning how to use the product
6. financing

   a. exchange
   b. borrow
   c. rent
   d. lease
   e. buy

7. service
   a. advice
   b. procurement
   c. delivery
   d. installation
   e. additional functions
   f. maintenance/Care
   g. disposal/Replacement

Ultimately, the user decides emotionally, which product he prefers. This happens no matter how intensively he has considered the arguments beforehand. Because the user ultimately decides in favour of a product for emotional and not rational reasons, engineers and designers cannot take over the design of a product. The engineering designer lacks the understanding for desire-creating and purchase-deciding emotional impulses of products. The user does not buy the best product, the user buys the product with the smallest compromise. The compromise is the important component for the decision to buy a product. When designing a new product, it helps the designer to know what compromises the user has made with current products. With this knowledge, the designer can channel his innovative power and work out a product that again creates a high desirability for the user.

Responsibility is assumed with every project.

The designer works result-oriented and tries to achieve this goal in a reasonable time. A designer does not design a me-too product, he strives to improve a product in at least one of the following ways:

1. the user
   a. solve problems and not create new ones in the process
   b. arouse emotions
   c. create experiences
   d. ecology (conserving resources, reducing environmental pollution)
   e. build brand awareness among users or sharpen
   f. satisfy curiosity

2. towards the client
   a. development time
   b. development costs
   c. production costs
   d. brand core
   e. distribution structure

Finding relationships can happen in the most diverse, even contradictory ways. The recognition and the resulting intentional composing and combining the relationships is the decisive formative step. Facing the effect of the design, taking it further, optimising it and presenting it as a coherent result rounds off the design process and present it as a conclusive result.

Details of a successful design process:

As different as the tasks may be in detail, the path that the designer takes when designing a new product is the same.

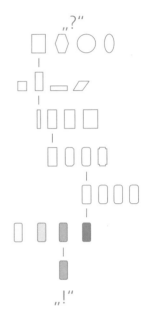

1. develop problem awareness
   a. identify problems
   b. describe problems
   c. prioritise problems
2. develop solutions
   a. develop variants
   b. present variants realistically
   b. evaluate variants
   c. optimise variants
3. presentation in a team
   a. evaluate several solutions in plenary
   b. evaluate together
   c. detail the task and go to go to point 2
   d. confirm task and go to go to point 4
4. sample
   a. final design is created
   b. handover to development or design department
5. support
   a. coordinate details in the development and design phase with the team
   b. confirm construction
6. redesign
   a. identify weaknesses
   b. record changed framework conditions
   c. go to point 2

Requirements of the development partners

A product is not developed by designers alone, but it emerges from a network of different competences that formulate contradictory requirements:
- sales
- marketing
- design
- manufacturing
- corporate management
- user

By disclosing the respective requirements of the individual areas, the designer can show the consequences of individual requirements in the appearance of the product by means of design variants. In this process, the designer acts as a mediator and project driver. The designer's negotiating skills enable him to take the decisive position in product development.

User requirement

Compromises made during development in favour of different requirements must not lead to the user not understanding the product. A product that appears to the user to have no structure or a chaotic structure will not be successful with the corresponding target group.

The user does not tolerate compromises in appearance. The user only recognises consistent products as desirable products.

Good design is consistent.

Too many cooks spoil the soup. At this point, we are not talking about constraints, but about the external impact of a product.

For a convincing design, there needs to be a designer who leads the project, who holds the decision-making authority according the "appearance" of the product. If this is not the case, the readability of a product suffers. The product will appear contradictory, too many different intentions will be visible in the product. The result is that the target group will not understand the meaning of the product.

For designers it is a balancing act how far they allow criticism from outside to flow into their work, because design is also teamwork.

There are designers who formulated their own enduring values and thus made their procedures more transparent for all those involved, two examples are
  – the *Ten Theses on design* by Dieter Rams
  – the *Vignelli Canon* by Massimo Vignelli
Most designers who have been active for many years draw on a wealth of experience without documenting it in guidelines.

The designer must always ask himself: Is the intention pursued with the design recognisable as the desired effect on the user?

The designer is a cultural creator

Design is a human science!
The designer is obliged to the user to design a product that fulfils his needs. The framework in which it fulfils this task is made up of chewing, technical and other requirements.

To achieve this, the designer must combine the following skills:

- — empathy for his target group
- — recognising and understanding requirements
- — question existing solutions constructively
- — identify problems
- — develop problem-solving, forward-looking visions
- — develop user-oriented formal solutions
- — implementing proposed solutions

Furthermore, a designer needs the ability to present ideas and concepts to others in a comprehensible and convincing way. Be it through sketches, with the help of models or other aids.

Because the designer develops several equivalent solutions, he must be able to decide on one version and implement it consistently.

The position of the designer

Designers are innovators. Innovations are erratic developments that can only be planned to a very limited extent. The development of innovative concepts cannot be brought about with previously defined work processes. They require time and erratic associations, which a designer brings about by means of the most diverse working methods.

The designer always develops several different concepts. These are jointly evaluated in development teams for their innovation potential. This means that the designer's design process precedes the development process. Due to the scope of the design work, the designer is in direct exchange with the most important decision-makers of a company.

If a product needs a facelift only, the designer speaks of styling. Styling is the aesthetic elaboration of the outer appearance of a product. It does not interfere with the functionality of a product. Styling satisfies fashionable needs. For functioning technical substructures, this is a legitimate procedure, because other user needs have already been taken into account in the preceding model series. Styling is a sub-area of design, it is positioned behind development, these projects are led by a project manager.

Designers create new products in the design phase before the development and construction phases. If new products are developed technically first and the designer is used as a stylist. In this case, a holistic user experience is not taken into account and the success of a product will be very much dependent on chance.

**Designers always observe their surroundings
with an alert eye.**

Unfortunately, the designer does not know today what will be
important tomorrow, so he must observe his environment and
search for sources of inspiration. A designer is permanently
curious about new things.

1. technical sources
   a. production process
   b. problems with existing products
   c. innovations
   d. materials
2. market
   a. purchasing behaviour
   b. competitors
   c. distribution or sales problems
3. within the company
   a. further development of the brand
   b. personnel changes
   c. general conditions in production and assembly
4. design sources
   a. observations of nature
   b. social observations
   c. technical knowledge transfer
   d. sensory material properties
   e. narrative elements
5. culture
   a. art in general
   b. fashion/trends

c. observation of the open discourse

6. society
   a. social developments
   b. economic and ecological developments
   c. development of interest groupings

7. problem awareness
   a. critical reflection
   b. develop descriptive adjectives,
      describing problems or solutions
   c. Identify inconsistencies

8. research
   a. technology
   b. market
   c. user

9. perceptual skills

...

Most solution approaches arise from transfer services and the subsequent adaptation to one's own task. A designer is particularly well suited for this, because his competence is fed by activities in the most diverse fields, so that he can initiate and implement knowledge and technology transfers.

In the context of digitalisation, traditional digital departments in which digital competences and possibilities are combined with classic product worlds and further developed into new solutions.

The constuctor

has the certainty that what he designs is based on rational requirements, according to which he can continue to optimise in the future.

The constructor's goal:
1. to guarantee technical functionality in the best possible way
2. to make production as economical as possible

Requirements for the designer:
1. compliance with industrial standards
2. specifications of the legislator
3. safety specifications
4. specifications
5. cost and benefit calculations

Tools of the constructor:
1. mechanical laws
2. physics, biology, chemistry

Result of the constructor:
An optimal result within the framework of the requirements

Collaboration of the constructor:
1. production
2. design

The designer

strives to unite the requirements from the individual areas in a way that is fair to the target groups.

Aim of the designer:
1. to recognise the wishes and needs of the user.
2. to consider constructive possibilities and impossibilities take into account

Requirements for the designer:
1. development of innovative products
2. adapting products to suit the target group
3. improvement of the current situation
4. CI/CD of a brand
5. presenting ideas in a vivid and comprehensible way

Tools of the designer:
1. mechanical laws
2. physics, biology, chemistry
3. business administration
4. psychology
5. sociology

Result of the designer:
The designer develops products for a specific scenario and tries to adapt the products optimally to these scenarios.

Collaboration of the designer:

1. management
2. marketing
3. development
4. construction
5. production
6. sales
7. users
8. service

The artist

follows a self-imposed intention, for which he can use anything that stimulates the viewer´s imagination and leads to new insights.

Aim of the artist:
   1. to develop new possibilities of expression.
   2. the creation of a change of
      perspective that leads to new insights
      for the viewer

Requirements for the artist:
   1. development of unique selling points

Tools of the artist
   1. every material
   2. the concept

Result of the artist:
For the artist, the result is freely selectable
   1. single piece
   2. small series of handicrafts
   3. serial production methods of all kinds
   4. oldest and most modern production
      methods

Collaboration of the artist:
   1. producers (who realise his idea)
   2. assistants (who realise his idea)
   3. art market, gallery owner
   4. patrons, art collectors

CONCLUSION

In the previous pages, an overview of the factors influencing Gestalt was given. These were summarised under the term context. It was made clear that these factors are at the same time framework conditions and design tools of a designer.

In order for a designer to be able to begin his work at all, he starts a new project by analysing the project's own context; in the course of the project, he modulates this context according to the further research. The more aware a designer is of the individual parameters, the more accurate and successful the product will be. In the process, the design phase for development partners also becomes comprehensible to all involved and the entire design and development process is shortened.

The design parameters are like a network of relationships, a net that is laid over a blank. In the design phase, it is adjusted several times and thus controls the form finding and the form evaluation.

A well-developed network of relationships serves as a decision-making aid and as argumentation for finding the shape of the new product. Individual concepts can be compared transparently and viable ideas can be distinguished from those that are not.

In order to do this, the designer must have the empathic, creative and diplomatic skills to incorporate the possibilities and limitations that exist in the context into a new product. Furthermore, the designer has to reconcile the complexity of human perception and human behaviour patterns with the applicability and manufacturability of a product.

A further thought shows the limits of this understanding of design. If any number of parameters are named and connected with each other, the idea of developing software and turning a computer into a designer is obvious.

However, the computer is not capable of understanding and evaluating variants, because it can only grasp human behaviour patterns in a mesh-like way and cannot imitate the contradictory nature of human beings. These are characteristics that will continue to be reserved for humans.

In a design, relationships also arise that are not planned beforehand, but which influence the readability of a design. A computer can neither recognise nor evaluate these new relationships. It lacks the intelligence described in the book.

It turns out that the human abilities
  – developing and evaluating relationships
  – intuition and creativity
are human qualities that cannot be copied.

The computer as a tool will be able to quickly generate variants for the designer, developed from requirements previously defined by humans. Thus, the designer remains the creative and directional master of the situation.

Successful designers
  – observe
  – develop
  – evaluate
  – optimise
their design work in the context of the products.

Architekturgeometrie	Pottmann, Asperl, Hofer, Kilian
Bilder des Wissens	Olaf Breidbach
Der Geheime Code	Priya Hemenway
Der Mensch und seine Zeichen	Adrian Frutiger
Der Modulor	Le Corbusier
Der Modulor 2	Le Corbusier
Design	Lindwell, Holden, Butler
Design for the Real world	Victor Papanek
Die Gegenstandslose Welt	Kasimir Malewitsch
Die Geschichte der Schönheit	Umberto Eco
Die vier Bücher der Architektur	Andrea Palladio
Der Vignelli Kanon	Massimo Vignelli
Entwerfen und Darstellen	Roland Knauer
Entwurfskultur und Gesselschaft	Gui Bonsiepe
Essays über Kunst und Künstler	Wassily Kandinsky
Farbenlehre	Harald Küppers
Freiräum(en):	Hans Loidl
Entwerfen als Landschaftsarchitektur	
Generative Gestaltung	Bohnacker, Groß, Laub, Lazzeroni
Geometry of Design	Kimberly Elam
Grundlagen des Entwerfens	Ermel, Brauneck, Molter, Novak
Grundlagen der Gestaltung,	André Vladimir Heiz
Kompendium des Industrie-Designs	Heinz Habermann
Mensch und Raum	Otto Friedrich Bollnow

IMPRESSUM

The Deutsche Nationalbibliothek lists this publication
in the Deutsche Nationalbibliografie; detailed bibliographic
data are available on the Internet at http://dnb.dnb.de

ISBN 978-3-7212-1020-0
© 2023 Niggli, imprint of Braun Publishing AG, Salenstein
www.niggli.ch

1st edition 2023

Translation, Editing,
Graphic concept, Layout: Mike Ambach
Proofreading: Sandra Ellegiers

ACKNOWLEDGEMENTS

This project went on for a very long time.
As simple and clear as it now (hopefully) appears,
it was not at all in the beginning. It had to be liberated,
reduced and sorted so that the essentials could appear
self-evident, clear and simple.

So now we have a small reference work.
In the hope that other designers will be
inspired to discover and develop further
building blocks.

In order to make this possible, I would like to
thank a publisher who let me do it and whose
helpful staff contributed significantly to the script
becoming a book.

In particular, I would like to thank those close
to me for all their constructive criticism, their
suggestions and for their time, patience and
effort:

Birgit Ludwig-Fischer, designer, lecturer and partner
Roland Knauer, professor
Ludger Vlatten, art collector and dear friend
Martin Wirsing, professor